Praise for *The Pursuit of Home*

"*The Pursuit of Home* is an excellent guide for anyone looking to buy a home. Scott Harris's smart, practical tips, expert real estate knowledge, and genuine passion for helping buyers will prepare you to move through the process with ease and walk away with a home you love."

—Barbara Corcoran, Shark on ABC's
Shark Tank and Founder, Corcoran Group

"A marvelously useful guide for those who dare pursue their dream of owning a home in America. It exposes not only the slings and arrows of the purchase process, but also the emotional pleasures and ultimately financial benefits of homeownership."

—Hipolito "Paul" Roldan, former President and CEO,
Hispanic Housing Development Corporation

"*The Pursuit of Home* is the best real estate guide available. Harris demystifies the real estate market and helps readers understand how they can make the most of their home buying experience. Do yourself a favor and read *The Pursuit of Home* before embarking on your own pursuit of a home."

—Kristin Jordan, Luxury Real Estate Advisor
and National Housing Expert

"Buying a home can be one of the most stressful things we voluntarily do, and other guides simply don't cover the roller coaster of the experience. *The Pursuit of Home* by Scott Harris clarifies every step of the real estate buying process, helps you make smarter home-buying decisions, and ensures you're prepared to find the home of your dreams. Follow Scott Harris's advice—you will be so glad you did."

—Mary Morrissey, Founder, Brave Thinking Institute

"*The Pursuit of Home* finally illuminates the emotional side of buying a home—an overdue topic in real estate. What we see on social media and reality TV is far from reality. This book brings meaning and real insight to a life-changing journey."

—Chris Heller, Founder, OJO Labs; former CEO, Keller
Williams Realty; and Nationally Bestselling Author

"Most people in search of their American dream have a vision that includes owning their own home. With *The Pursuit of Home*, Scott Harris opens a door for more Americans to make that dream a reality. He demystifies a complex process and provides the counsel that first-time homebuyers need as they navigate a life-changing experience.

The Pursuit of Home will allow more Americans to own the home of their dreams by answering their questions and offering support through one of the most consequential experiences of their lives. By providing a strategic and empathetic approach to the practical and emotional experience of the home-buying process, Scott Harris is a true advocate of the first-time homebuyer."

—Marc H. Morial, President and CEO, National Urban League

"Scott Harris's new book about home ownership stands out not simply because it's practical and insightful, but also because it's extremely well written. Reading *The Pursuit of Home* is like stumbling upon an exquisite little restaurant that you didn't know could exist, one that satisfies hungers you didn't realize you had. In this case, the hunger is to have a sense of creative control about how you find a home that's right for you and your finances. Harris is equal parts coach, business advisor, and therapist as he walks you through the process of envisioning what you want, and then attaining it. There's not another book like it!"

—Michael Urtuzuástegui Melcher, Author, *Your Invisible Network*

"Scott Harris is your dedicated real estate guide. He is committed to your needs before, during, and long after the sale. His client-focused approach has made him a leading real estate professional for decades. Now, for the first time, Scott shares his insights and strategies, built on a foundation of trust with hundreds of repeat clients and over a billion dollars in sales."

—Brady Johns, *Wall Street Journal* Bestselling
Author, *Flip-Flops and Fortunes*

THE PURSUIT OF HOME

The Pursuit of Home

Home

A Real Estate Guide
to Achieving the
American Dream

Scott Harris

MATT HOLT

Matt Holt Books
An Imprint of BenBella Books, Inc.
Dallas, TX

MATT HOLT ▦▦ BenBella

Matt Holt is an imprint of BenBella Books, Inc.
8080 N. Central Expressway
Suite 1700
Dallas, TX 75206
benbellabooks.com
Send feedback to feedback@benbellabooks.com

BenBella and *Matt Holt* are federally registered trademarks.

Printed in the United States of America
10 9 8 7 6 5 4 3 2 1

Library of Congress Control Number: 2025016169
ISBN 9781637747476 (hardcover)
ISBN 9781637747483 (electronic)

Editing by Katie Dickman
Copyediting by Michael Fedison
Proofreading by Rebecca Maines and Sarah Vostok
Indexing by Elise Hess
Text design and composition by PerfecType, Nashville, TN
Interior illustrations by Maria Dzvonyk
Cover design by Brigid Pearson
Cover image © Adobe Stock / Olena Rudo [AI generated]
Printed by Lake Book Manufacturing

For my brother Michael

CONTENTS

Prologue
Homeward Bound

Trumpet Girl: I heard you come from a broken home.
Animal: Yeah, I broke it myself.
—The Muppet Show, *Season 1, Episode 5*

Broken Homes

At the end of 2014, I paused to reflect on my career in real estate. Financially speaking, I had just had my best year. I had a wonderful wife and two daughters. My wife and I owned a home that we loved. Yet I had never been less happy, professionally speaking. I was utterly burned out. I had gone through four assistants in four years, not to mention the revolving door of agents working for me who seemed to quit every December. Either a breakdown was in my future or I was already there. Something had to change. But what?

With 12 years of selling residential property in New York City under my belt, I thought I had an inkling of what it took to be a good real estate agent. That was probably because I had started out as such a bad one. Choosing this vocation had been just another spontaneous move in a string of unconsidered life decisions. For example, I wasn't aware that the typical earnings of a first-year agent were only $32,000—40% below what an average working person was earning in the United States at that time. It wouldn't have mattered, though. Even that was a princely sum compared to my past employment history. And if my career wasn't destined to intertwine with real estate, I had been a lifelong spectator. My father operated a wholesale hardware business out of a commercial warehouse he owned. Naturally, tenants, leases, and property management were ever-present dinner table conversations. Later in my childhood, my mother became the marketing director for the New Orleans affiliate of a national real estate brokerage firm. She spoke the language of renovations and design and aspiration. I would eventually work part-time as a receptionist in her office the summer before college and absorb the energetic rush of agents closing residential deals.

It wasn't just learning by osmosis. By the time I got my salesperson's license at the age of 28, I had unknowingly assembled a stack of skills tailor-made for real estate. The seeds of entrepreneurship, or at least hustling, had been planted during my middle school years. My best friend's mother, who was the tour manager for the world-famous Preservation Hall Jazz Band during that period, took us away during a school break and let us—two giddy 12-year-olds—work the merchandise booth during intermissions. A pop-up nacho stand I opened at a seventh-grade fair only stoked this fire. Winning top prize for selling the most raffle tickets at school the following year was further confirmation I was on to something. I folded in the lessons of hospitality—an underappreciated skill set in the world of real estate—garnered from a slew of restaurant jobs I worked before and after college. And during my undergraduate years, I sold program ads and hawked concert tickets for my college a cappella group on the main campus thoroughfare every fall and spring, yelling at and charming passersby until they stopped and pulled money out of their pockets.

Before long, I was running an actual business for my band in Boston. Under the stage lights, I was listening, mimicking, and blending my voice in harmony, and trying to make people feel good. On the road and off, armed with a cell phone, a laptop, and dial-up internet, I addressed objections, handled rejections, negotiated our fees, and tackled our booking calendar. The results included more than a thousand performances while opening for late '90s boy bands such as 98 Degrees, NSYNC, and others—and a near-miss on a major-label record deal.

Entrepreneurship and marketing skills are foundational for a salesperson in any industry. However, in addition to the ability to map out a tour, I had also developed the soft skills I have found to be most critical to success in residential real estate: understanding people, empathizing with what they have gone through, and knowing how to get them out of their own way. You see, before I left home at 18, I had moved between my parents' two houses nearly *500* times as part of their joint custody arrangement. What came with that was a desperate need to keep the peace between them that converted my natural curiosity into highly attuned vigilance outside the home too. That meant studying facial expressions and body language, sniffing for signs of the slightest disagreements between people everywhere, and developing the resourcefulness to resolve them. I never questioned whether anything was possible or not, or whether there was a right way of doing it. If something needed to be done, I just forged ahead and figured things out. There was no other option, really, because it seemed that my life was at stake. These were the unexpected upsides of being a people pleaser.

On the other hand, buyers and sellers crave confident leadership. Mine emerged on the football field, starting with a high school coach who believed in me when I was a scrawny 140-pound freshman. I paid that inspiration forward when I became one of the team's captains in my senior year. Along with Cooper Manning (and his younger brother and future Hall of Fame–quarterback Peyton Manning), we led a team to a 12–2 record and a playoff run that he still talks about today.

Eventually, motivation of this sort became a formal area of study in a sense. My college course load of history and psychology brought me to the intersection of where human beings and their stories collide. I became an even keener observer of human behavior and decision-making at its most irrational, random, and complex.

The path from broke touring musician to successful real estate agent was paved with loss as well, and not just as a child of divorce. September 11, 2001, as it turns out, produced other unreported casualties of a sort: My band's biggest album release was on that same tragic Tuesday. The implosion of six people's dreams does not register on the same scale as the murder of 3,000 innocent souls, but it's still devastating when it's happening to you.

It was 9/11 that also prompted my move to New York. And my struggles to make ends meet in those early days packed plenty more compassion into my tool kit. I couch surfed, then shared a studio apartment with a childhood buddy to save money. I saw a glimmer of my future success when I started as a rental agent. But I also hated myself for being *really, really* good at closing deals in what was real estate's dirty back alley back then.

Everything changed when I put my set of skills into practice doing apartment sales. My priority shifted from closing a deal at any cost to delivering what restaurateur and author Will Guidara calls "unreasonable hospitality." I unlocked a new ability to operate on an intuitive, emotional level. My business expanded, but this ability also led me into a cottage industry of matchmaking that at first seemed unrelated to real estate. Like the best bartenders, I was the person with whom everyone opened up. I had flashes of awareness about who, or what, might save their day. For example, I matched a credit card processing firm with its biggest client to date. I connected a philanthropy to a massive new donor. I found college graduates what would be the first line on their future résumés. Almost on cue, clients and acquaintances also began referring me to their friends who needed new homes. I was helping people find their place in the world, figuratively and literally.

But somewhere along the line, I had lost my way. I almost gave up on residential real estate entirely during that soul-searching period in 2014 I mentioned. Instead, I began to rebuild myself and my team from the ground up. I sought out a variety of business coaches, signed up for too many self-improvement programs, read one self-help book after another, and concentrated on creating a business that I would love and a life that I loved at the same time. Things began to improve, slowly at first, then all at once, as they say. I soon realized that buying a home with my wife had done real work in healing the wounds of my childhood. This moment of clarity marked the true launch of the residential real estate team I run today.

These revelations, and others, also allowed me to articulate what I have come to see as my team's sacred mission: to empower people to fulfill their dreams through real estate. *The Pursuit of Home* grew out of a genuine desire to share what led to my clients' successes—and what might lead to yours. I had already been writing a blog on New York's real estate market for 15 years, which turned out to be good practice for writing a book. But I couldn't have predicted what it would turn into.

I'm thrilled to share it with you now.

CHAPTER 1

Happy Hunting

A New Blueprint

"Home wasn't built in a day."
—Jane Sherwood Ace

The Hero's Journey Begins

Welcome home.

This is a book about the American Dream. Whoever you are, and wherever you live, there is a high likelihood that yours includes owning a home. The day you buy it may very well be the best day of your life, after your wedding or the birth of your children. Homeownership, you could say, is the key to a good life.

It's not just Barbie who has been living in her Dreamhouse since 1962. More than 65% of Americans are in that club. They know the pride that homeownership confers. If you don't own a home yet, or are looking for a new one, how do you picture it? A white picket fence, a gleaming garage, a backyard with big mature trees, a wraparound porch with rocking chairs, an open front door to greet guests with a big smile on your face? Perhaps in your version, a child pokes her head out from behind your legs to catch a glimpse at whoever has arrived for a visit. You can almost smell the freshly cut grass. More cows than people and more gnats than nightlife might feature prominently in your dreams. Or perhaps you conjure up a view of Central Park from your living room, or a scene of laughing in front of a D.C. rowhouse, outside a San Francisco Victorian, or on a brownstone stoop, surrounded by quirky neighbors and James Beard Award–winning eateries.

Somewhere along the line, house hunting became a national obsession. Home ownership has, in an annual poll starting in 1975, garnered more votes than marriage as the ticket to paradise. Fast-forward to today, and Americans enjoy touring properties not only in person, but online or on television. We react with a flood of hearts to our friends' "We've moved!" posts on social media. We can't get enough of kitchen finishes or cabanas—or their demolition. We gawk at the curated lives of the rich and famous, and at their agents making deals over fancy lunches, all in ultra-high definition. The National

Association of Realtors®, or NAR, tracked more than six million home sales in 2021, nearly one-third of them purchased by first-time buyers. While the intervening years' transaction statistics have not reached this high-water mark, millions are still competing to purchase a home. You might be one of them, now or very soon.

But these statistics don't address how the thought of buying a home makes you *feel*. Your relationship with real estate is not straightforward—not at all. At every turn, you are reminded that this is the biggest investment you will ever make. Talking heads and agents drone on about mortgage preapprovals, financial statements, offer sheets, and down payments. The pressure builds with headlines that hype the housing market and its whipsawing interest rates. From what your neighbors paid for their homes, to estimates of what every house on the block is worth minute-to-minute, learning quickly becomes information overload.

People love the idea of owning a home, but the process of buying one can be emotionally bruising. We already know this. It is reliably ranked among the most traumatic events in our lives, next to death, divorce, and major illness. Why so? Because the contours of real estate deals do not look anything like those featured in an Instagram post, billboard, or reality television program. Because real estate books out there forget to mention that, in the thick of it, no one acts rationally, certainly not as rationally as you might believe. Deep down, we know that buying a home is more than a transaction. It is among the biggest transitions of our lives.

Like the other stressful transitions listed above, you can run from real estate, but you cannot hide from it forever. In all likelihood, you have spent nearly every single night of your life under a roof. Home is where we seek to satisfy many of our essential wants and desires. Your home sits at the intersection of everything you have done and all that you have been.

When life brings change, your needs change too. A gap forms between where you are and where you want to be. This is both a physical and a *meta*physical where. The places in which your life has taken place are, in many ways, inseparable from the memories you carry with you. You may think you're looking for a brick-and-mortar house. What you seek, however, is but a concrete marker of a bigger mission: your life, lived to the fullest. The pursuit of homeownership, then, is a wonderful, exciting journey upon which to embark. All the same, like any other rite of passage, it is fraught with fear and mistrust.

🏠 🏠 🏠

About three years ago, I flew to Las Vegas to speak at a real estate conference. There, jet-lagged and awake at 3 AM the night before my presentation, I watched *Joseph Campbell and The Power of Myth*, an old series of interviews between journalist Bill Moyers and author Joseph Campbell that debuted on PBS in 1988. Campbell walked Moyers through centuries of religion and a variety of cultures to explain the same story structure he found in each of them, what he had famously dubbed the "hero's journey." You may not have heard the phrase, but you know the content. It is the storyline of every Disney movie. It underpins every Greek tragedy and Shakespearean play. It is the scaffolding of every legend or epic, and even many biblical tales. The hero's journey encapsulates the human experience.

Campbell first wrote about the stages of the hero's journey in *The Hero with a Thousand Faces* in 1949. In sweeping terms, he described them as "a separation from the world, a penetration to some source of power, and a life-enhancing return." While the protagonists of fairy tales are larger than life and perhaps even exceptionally gifted, Campbell's main point was that the same redemption "is hidden within us all, only waiting to be known and rendered into life." As I listened to him speak rapturously about the connection between myths and reality, I had an aha moment. There's more to a house than its investment potential, and much more than its practical, personal usefulness. There is magic in homeownership. And the outline Campbell described was the homebuying journey, just wearing different clothes.

Homebuyers like you are the heroes. You begin your search for a new home unsure, anxious, fearful, weighed down, banged up, and in desperate need of assistance. To navigate this burdensome environment, you'll enlist all the help you can get. Enter real estate agents, whom you may know as salespeople, brokers, or perhaps Realtors® if they are members of the National Association of Realtors (NAR). Great agents create the conditions so that every conversation elicits an insight, and every insight gets you closer to home. I no longer even saw myself as a real estate agent, but more like one of those spirits in the myths of ancient civilizations. Wasn't every buyer or seller in need of the same careful guidance?

This book was written to reflect the real-life roller coaster that is buying a home, and how you will become a better person for having hopped on for a ride. Here are its stages: You'll know that it's time to move, and yet will want to refuse the call (chapter 2: "No One Can Time the Real Estate Market"). Then you will meet, and select, the real estate professionals—your mentors and guides—for your journey (chapter 3: "Listings Aren't Enough"). For better or worse, you'll have to venture out from your old house, and into a world you think you know—but don't really (chapter 4: "There Is No Free Will in Real Estate"). From there, you'll face your initial real estate tests (chapter 5: "Every House Becomes a Guest House"). Like landing a plane, you'll begin your initial descent to your dream house (chapter 6: "Make Your Own Housing Market"). Only then, when things are looking pretty good, will you face your biggest predicament (chapter 7: "House Training"). It is after this conquest that you finally receive your reward—you get to close!—and dash down the road of domesticity (chapter 8: "You Can Go Home Again"). Finally, your dream home offers you the freedom to live a new, and bigger, life (chapter 9: "The Launch Pad").

I am honored to accompany my clients on their journey and guide them to positive outcomes. By the time you reach the closing table, you should be delighted with your new home too. At least that's the idea. But although more people are using real estate agents than ever before, fewer buyers and sellers are rosy about their experiences. In fact, the research spits out truly abysmal feedback. Nearly three-quarters of recent buyers interviewed expressed remorse when their transaction is complete, along with significant dissatisfaction over home size, location, and the speed at which they felt compelled to make a decision.

Adding to this remorse and dissatisfaction, those looking to buy a home today have never harbored a less optimistic outlook, informed by a particularly uncooperative climate in which to do so. For starters, more than half of all apartments in the United States are owned by institutional investors. One in four single-family homes were snapped up by corporations in 2023. Some believe that, without legislation, investment funds could own as much as 40% of these properties within the next 10 years. Meanwhile, nearly a third of the largest properties in America are owned and underutilized by empty nesters—twice as many as are owned by millennials with young children. That's a mismatch with real consequences. For younger buyers, it means those homes with more bedrooms aren't hitting the market. Were that not enough, real estate industry lawsuit settlements are also rewriting the way agents do business, and impacting how we go about choosing our new living arrangements.

♠ ♠ ♠

With this state of affairs as a backdrop, then, it is worth exploring how anyone can achieve a happy ending to their story. Let's begin by addressing what is right under our noses: Buyers have never had more access to what's on the market, while giving less attention to the things that matter. They've been distracted by decades of Nancy Meyers movies and their impossibly beautiful houses, by curated Instagram property tours that ignore humans altogether, by home improvement shows that hardly feature a disagreement, and by television producers and their glammed-up agent "influencers" peddling a homebuying process that does not exist. John F. Kennedy remarked that "the great enemy of the truth is very often not the lie, deliberate, contrived and dishonest, but the myth, persistent, persuasive and unrealistic." He wasn't referring specifically to the house hunt, but your friends often mythologize their experience too. Except these myths omit the unpleasant, and necessary, parts of the hero's journey that Campbell has so well described.

All of this is to say that homebuyers have not been remotely prepared for the actual home search *before* they start looking. And few real estate agents have been prepared to manage the process properly. Combine all of these things, and the chasm between buyers' aspirations and their real-world results should not come out of the blue. However, these misinformed expectations have been silent killers, erasing the dreams of those who never make it to the closing table, and serving as an impediment to those who do.

The Blueprint for This Book

Would you prefer to make smarter homebuying decisions? Do you want the process to be more enjoyable, satisfying, and successful? I will put it another way: What if the search for a home could give you so much more than you thought? That is a lot better than moving and still getting nowhere, isn't it?

I'm sorry to say that the preexisting buyer guides and reality television shows out there will not get you any closer to the home you want. In truth, the biggest secret of homebuying has been hiding in plain sight. The home search is, at its heart, a path of personal growth. And because so many people seek to buy a home during their lifetime, it is also the most readily available, and least painful, access we have to that growth.

This book doesn't just map the hero's journey onto your home-buying experience, however. It offers you a completely different and better method of homebuying. It will help you unlearn everything you thought you knew about real estate because almost none of it will be helpful when you actually go to buy a home.

Through writing this book, I have reverse engineered the house hunt. What I'm offering you is a step-by-step, heart-centered guide to finding the right home in the most effective and nourishing way possible—a way that leaves you in love with your house, in line with your vision, and in love with your *life*. You benefit from the wisdom that can only come from closing thousands of deals—and watching twice that number fall apart. Only out of this vast ocean of failures have I been able to create what I named The Magnetic Method™. It's a proven system for buyers and sellers that helps you use real estate as a means to an end: You find a house, yes, but it also helps bring you and your wildest dreams together.

We will investigate how the most talented, hardworking high earners in the biggest city in America complete their incredibly complicated real estate deals. But why would their twists and turns apply to you, sitting on a bench in Buffalo, or a couch in Cleveland, or a sofa in San Jose? I'll paraphrase Frank Sinatra and say if you can make it there, you can make it anywhere. Are you renting and just thinking about what's next? New York has the highest concentration of renters in the United States. Are you a first-time buyer? Nowhere are the hurdles and barriers to entry higher than in New York City. Struggling to lock down a loan? Nowhere is it more back-breaking to get approval to buy, with high prices, stout competition, and the cooperative purchase process—a uniquely awful gauntlet buyers run through in my market. Experiencing the New York City real estate market has not only equipped me to be an excellent guide for you. Its trials and tribulations also perfectly encapsulate what your homebuying experience is likely to be, wherever you are.

Yes, the elements of the transaction itself will have a different order depending on where you live—I make sure to point out where— but the journey is otherwise identical. And while these tales are emotionally heightened, and likely more insane than anything you will encounter, my hope is that the typical pitfalls will feel far less overwhelming by comparison, and that my tried-and-true suggestions to embrace them, avoid them, or overcome them will feel even more achievable. Even better, you get to conjure up your own responses to them. Further, you will identify your shortcomings and identify someone who can help you address and minimize the risk of them negatively impacting your search.

I have seen the results of leaning in to my very different method of homebuying. The right home will positively influence every aspect of your life, from the sacred to the profane. My work has saved marriages. My buyers have written bestselling novels under their new roofs. Homes become the launching pads for newly found lives of purpose and passion. You, too, have within you the power to make your American Dream come true. Before making the most substantial financial investment of your life, what is the danger in making an investment in yourself?

Before we set out, I make these promises to you:

- You will be equipped to bring to light what you *really* want in your new home and be able to communicate it to others.
- Even if you are cautious and concerned about hiring a real estate agent, you will witness great real estate agents doing their work and learn how to find one suited to your unique needs and communication styles.
- You will have tools, tricks, and frameworks at your fingertips that will lead to a successful home purchase.
- You will encounter and get to practice the necessary soft skills to address the practical, emotional, ethical, and even spiritual challenges at each step of the homebuying process.

How does that sound?

🏠 🏠 🏠

Take a moment to be proud of yourself. Celebrate the work you have done to save enough to buy a home. That is no small feat. And before you decide that this journey must be stressful, here's a radical idea: You don't have to suffer one iota more than is necessary through this process. Decide instead that you're going to have fun.

One warning, though: It could also seem fun, not to mention tempting, to skip ahead, or skip around, or constantly look for short-cuts. To do so, however, will not help you. Because you're no longer watching the story. *You are the story.* It's no different from ignoring the directions when you're putting together a cabinet from IKEA. You will just have a wobbly cabinet in the end, along with a bunch of loose screws and other important, but unused, parts. Don't squander the opportunity to do this right. Because if you do, you will have no one else to blame when you don't love your house.

On the flip side, you may be thinking, *I'm not in a rush.* I regularly hear buyers (and sellers too) use that phrase. While you may say you're willing to wait for the right property at the right price, you mean something else: You want to remain in control. That's okay. This book was designed to put you in the driver's seat, even as it asks you to get out of your comfort zone. My advice? Do your best not to add any pressure to artificially speed up or slow down your search. Because finding your home will take as long as it takes.

The silver lining is there are no preparations required. Just show up with curiosity. A world of progress comes from even one incremental shift in your approach.

It's impossible not to have some difficulties—from moving your online search to real-world property visits, to unsuccessfully identifying your "must-haves," to hating every house you've viewed, to losing deal after deal, to obsessing over the idea that you can "time" the market, to keeping it together when you really love a house. No one posts about these land mines, nor will real estate websites point them out. But they are real. Consider the possibility that the biggest handicap to your success is staring back at you in the mirror. I won't just tell you that you'll get in your own way. I will show you again and again how you're likely to do it.

Can we just agree to get uncomfortable together? If so, repeat after me: *I want a house I love. It's out there waiting for me.* Take notice if you're shaken and stirred up by that statement, and especially if you're rolling your eyes at the second sentence. This really is a hero's journey, and you will get all the help you need. That is the point, really. You are never alone in your house hunt—not that you could do this alone if you tried. Speaking of not being alone, prepare yourself for unseen help. You can call it luck, synchronicity, the Force, the Universe, a Higher Power, or whatever you like. There's a lot more to real estate than meets the eye.

♠ ♠ ♠

Some more advice: While I know that it is fascinating to be a fly on the wall of multimillion-dollar mansions, this book is for anyone looking for a real *home*. I can imagine that from the outside, New York City's residential real estate appears like a surreal high-wire act, with unimaginably high prices. Its intrepid home seekers face unique obstacles such as cooperative apartments that scarcely exist anywhere else in the rest of the country, or the world. I promise you that these buyers put their pants on one leg at a time, just like you. If the numbers seem too high for your market (they certainly could; the average home price in America is, as of 2023, $412,000), just subtract a zero from any purchase price I mention, whenever you like.

And to the investment-minded out there, a warning: You won't find advice on how to "steal" a piece of property, nor will I divulge some heretofore secret method for ripping someone's face off in a negotiation. I won't treat a home, nor any buyers or sellers, like a piece of meat. In fact, this book is not geared to investors. I will only say this: Research, exotic financing, fixing and flipping, digging for deals, and making or saving money are meaningless if you forget that the most important home improvements you make are to yourself. Still, I must remind you not to take anything in this book to be financial or investment advice. You should always consult with your real estate agent and the professionals you have hired before committing to any home purchase.

Nevertheless, I'll go out of my way to explain the inner workings of deals for you, and the language around them. I don't mean to insult your intelligence, but I don't want to assume that you come in knowing all the real estate jargon either. Therefore, when there is a word or phrase with which you may not be familiar, I have strived mightily to include it in what I've dubbed "The Big Glossary of Real Estate," which you can find online—like the rest of the exercises, question-naires, and quizzes.[†] I intended this glossary to serve as a directory of as many relevant real estate terms as possible, and it even includes many terms not mentioned in the book. Take what is helpful for you.

⌂ ⌂ ⌂

In the pages ahead you'll read plenty of stories about my personal and professional setbacks as well as plenty of unfiltered drama, since within that conflict is where the real learnings reside. My clients are at least as complex and imperfect as homebuyers anywhere. It is like that scene in the 1999 romantic comedy *Notting Hill*. Each of us is also just a girl, standing in front of a boy, asking him to love her. Except the boy in this case is a house. Dare I say this might be the most compassionate tell-all you've ever read. To that end, I have altered my clients' names, and changed just enough of the details to keep them anonymous. I have also combined their experiences and stories—all of them true—here and there. The essential lessons of their journeys, however, remain intact.

If you're like most homebuyers, you will be skeptical about your prospects of success from time to time. This is normal. No proper hero thinks that she is the one to save the world. Certainly not at the beginning of the journey. But whenever your skepticism emerges, I want this question ringing in your ears: What is the downside of play-ing the homebuying game with a new set of rules?

---

† Find "The Big Glossary of Real Estate" at pursueyourhome.com/glossary.

CHAPTER 2

No One Can Time the Real Estate Market

Overcoming the Obstacles to Starting Your Search

"You don't have to go home but you can't stay here."
—Every bartender in America at closing time

The Call to Adventure

The house hunt, like the hero's journey, begins at the point of an epiphany: *I have to move.* This is the shift that sets everything else in motion. Like tectonic plates, our circumstances move unceasingly and imperceptibly over weeks, months, or years. These changes often do not register on your emotional seismograph. But then the dishes start trembling in the cupboard, a giant hole in the earth appears, and a mountain surges upward right outside your window. You don't notice anything until you do, seemingly, all at once. It is like being an adolescent on the other side of a growth spurt. The house seems smaller because you have physically become bigger.

If you ponder what life throws at you, one thing becomes clear. The universe operates at its own unpredictable pace. It could be anything from inheriting money from your eccentric aunt Rita to your landlord deciding to sell your rental house. It could begin with your parents downsizing to a retirement community across town and tossing you from the basement. Subtle, serious, or sublime, these changes rock us to our core. Yet they each have the potential to propel you along the path to your next home, if you can overcome your shaky first steps.

I say shaky because, unfortunately, on the heels of this epiphany is often a second thought: *I don't want to move.* Left to your own devices, you may not move at all, no matter how bad things are, or how wonderful things have just become. Because nothing will deflate your dreams faster than simply mobilizing for the house hunt. Let's look at the obstacles that threaten to keep you stuck in place, and how to overcome them—so you can start your search off on the right foot.

Moving Away or Moving Toward

We can group the catalysts behind most real estate transactions into two main categories: push and pull. There are those that push you away from your past, like the three Ds: death, divorce, and debt. Other pushes might include a breakup, a job loss, a lack of viable romantic prospects in your town, or—forget swiping left or right—falling out of love with where you live. Each may open your eyes to what is wrong, what is missing, what once was and cannot be again.

The second category of real estate motivators pull you toward a future, what could be *right* about something new. They might begin appearing in your subconscious. You know those dreams, in which you open a door in your living room that wasn't there before and you find an extra bedroom. They're trying to tell you something, aren't they? Other motivators begin with a chat at the end of the bar, and bloom into a love affair, an engagement ring, and a revelation that this merger of two lives no longer requires two home addresses. Perhaps you rented an Airbnb in the country for the summer, or moved into your cousin's country place in between jobs, and became obsessed with nature. Maybe the virtual workplace freed you to pursue your dream of relocating to the desert or the mountains full-time. A positive pregnancy test might induce a wholesale mindset makeover. That two-bedroom apartment you just moved into six months ago suddenly feels much, much smaller when your second child is on the way. Your readiness to move may quickly reach full-term too. All it takes is one chance comment, one encounter, one enchanted evening to open your eyes to entirely new possibilities, and goals you never deemed worthy of chasing before. Excitement is a tractor beam that locks onto you and will not let go.

♔ ♔ ♔

Being excited should be a good thing, right? The Oxford dictionary defines the word *excite* as "to make enthusiastic and eager." But look at the secondary definition of the word: "to stir up, to emotionally agitate, to set into motion." Behind every exciting life change lies the daunting prospect of the unknown.

It's the unknown, the dark side of excitement, that creates obstacles, obstacles that will weigh you down and, in truth, hold back most buyers from moving for a short time, or longer. We can divide them into three categories. I'll label them *inertia*, *negative judgment*, and *ambivalence*. Each requires a different strategy to begin to overcome them.

Inertia

Jacob and Lisa were only jolted out of their stupor after a vacation, the fog of their busy lives wiped clean, the unvarnished facts finally in front of them. Their family of four was jammed into a one-bedroom apartment. The sons slept on gym mats in the bedroom. They had a living room that doubled as an *American Ninja Warrior* obstacle course, and at bedtime, the pull-out couch became the parents' full-time bed. A question appeared: *What have we been doing?* They couldn't endure being mushed together any longer.

The antidote to inertia is clarity, which comes from either perspective or information. Beach vacations are good for perspective. Information, on the other hand, won't come to you on a lounge chair. You'll have to go out and find it. Diana Vasquez, New Jersey Realtor® and founder of the Spanish-language real estate education portal La Chapulina Verde, pointed out that more than one in four homebuyers in the United States last year speaks Spanish as their first language. She believes the only reason that the Hispanic community does not represent an even bigger piece of the buyer pie is due to a combination of information scarcity and information overload. Both have created inertia. One could say that the steps of the real estate transaction, along with the means of finding good agents, are getting lost in translation, literally, in this case, or figuratively. You've heard that information is power. Delivered effectively, it will begin to weaken inertia's hold.

Negative Judgment

It's no stretch to see why you might worry about people judging your decision to buy, and how those worries can become another major obstruction. Let's say, for example, that your work bonus or promotion means you can finally afford that bigger house. A celebratory occasion, indeed. But then you contemplate what might be uttered behind your back—*that must be nice*—will it cause you to second-guess yourself? Will you take action if it could create a wedge between you and your jealous family and friends? Or will you downplay your success instead?

Fear of negative judgment can kill almost anyone's enthusiasm. How do you set about counteracting this fear? Make a list of those friends, mentors, and family members you are certain won't judge you. And make a second list of those who will. Keep those on the second list at arm's length, at least for now.

Ambivalence

You can't exactly shield yourself from a spouse's reluctance, though. And your doubtful spouse could crush your fledgling dreams of moving. Take Julie and Brad. The blushing bride, still glowing from their wedding, was beyond eager at our intake meeting. Over the course of an hour, she excitedly dove into monologue after monologue about their tiny rental apartment and where they would create their life together. I sent them away with two take-home activities, and then exactly nothing happened. They never completed the balance sheet I gave them, nor did they call the mortgage broker I recommended to get their preapproval in place. They just vanished. I was not taken aback or even remotely offended, though. Brad had said nothing during our entire meeting. What often holds back even the most charged-up couples is that they aren't on the same page. One is excited, and the other is ambivalent. James Clear, in his book *Atomic Habits*, calls this divide "motion versus action." Motion is the result of a flurry of excitement embedded with fear and ambivalence. Action implies something more meaningful and constructive and confident. When, or if, Brad and Julie reemerge, it will be as a far less honeymoon-y version of themselves, but a version that has overcome their collective ambivalence, ready to take action.

David and Zina could have been homeowners the day after they got married. Their parents let them choose between a lavish wedding or a down payment for a house. Like most young couples, they opted for the party, and a New York rental apartment. What would you have done? Years later, when I met them, they were again weighing their options. They and their two children had moved into her parents' house in the suburbs, as many people did during the pandemic, and were able to save a down-payment-sized amount by living rent-free for more than a year. Yet again, rather than buy, they moved back to the city, just into a larger rental apartment than before. What had not moved was their ambivalence.

This rental-first mentality can be alluring, even with more than enough money for a purchase. Leslie and Stewart, for instance, had been renting a series of apartments for 20 years when we met. Before we could even begin discussing why they were contemplating a purchase after so long, Stewart emerged as the ambivalent one. He went so far as to call real estate a "sucker's game." Let's just say Stewart was not on board with Leslie's vision. Ambivalence is a tough roadblock to maneuver around without deft guidance. We'll come back to them in a later chapter and share their happy ending.

🏠 🏠 🏠

One last thing about renting. Not only does it display ambivalence, but also an impermanence I have never heard better articulated than in my hometown during my childhood. New Orleans has many regionalisms, from the most famous "Who Dat" chants for its football team to its real estate–related "shotgun houses." The one that struck me most, though, was when someone would ask, "Where do you stay?" Distinguish this question from the typical one, "Where do you *live*?" Were housing arrangements so fleeting, so ephemeral, that one could only be expected to know where they might be sleeping that night, or in the near term? That's not the point of view of someone bullish on their future.

This particular phrasing has stuck in my memory because of my own upbringing. On any given week, I could barely keep track of where I might be staying. Nor did my nomadic reality end when I no longer lived in my parents' homes full-time. For the six years after college, my home was more of a mailing address, since I was traveling in a 33-foot RV and staying in hotels more than half the year while performing across the country with my band.

Any landlord will tell you that renters do not treat a home the same way an owner would. While they refer to a rental property's accelerated physical wear and tear, I'm thinking more about how casually I acted in general before I bought a home, even when facing important decisions. Nothing seemed that consequential. I could never look down on you, or anyone, for renting, or "staying by their momma's," or couch surfing when that is all that's affordable. Just be careful that renting your home doesn't become leasing your *life*. It gets thornier over the years to stop thinking like a renter; it's a habit you'll want to break as soon as you can.

🏠 🏠 🏠

You may be wondering where a real estate agent fits into tearing down these self-imposed fortifications. Couldn't I have more effectively demonstrated the financial upside of buying versus renting? After all, there is nothing like homeownership that offers the same elegant, color-by-numbers, tax-efficient, one-mortgage-payment-at-a-time system for building wealth. This idea has unleashed an enthusiasm so contagious that it turns entire neighborhoods around, and brings cities back from the brink of bankruptcy. But will any of that necessarily move your needle? If either you, your spouse, or both of you are too overwhelmed or too worried about what people will say, no amount of salesmanship is going to change your mind. Believe me, I've tried.

For certain, you don't need to have a partner to rent or buy a home, nor to stumble out of the starting blocks. If you wish, you can do that all by yourself, even though you'll be living in the same metaphorical halfway house with everyone else. It's an effort to shed these burdens alone or in pairs.

🏠 🏠 🏠

Holding On, or Letting Go

I started this chapter by saying that the house hunt begins when you realize that you have to move, then shuts down temporarily when that competing voice says, *I don't want to.* That voice can be a siren call, and it can dash you against the rocks. You know who shares your pain? Those who have to sell before buying. It's so obvious as to be unnecessary, don't you think? Any real estate agent, including me, could write an entire book about sellers who wrestled with the decision to let go of their home. Just know that you are in good company.

Have you ever found yourself incapable of doing the activities necessary to move your dreams forward, even at the peak of your enthusiasm? Don't sweat how little progress you might have made so far toward your dream home. I've laid out a sampling of what has kept you in neutral, but there is a solution to overcome whatever interference stands in your way. You just need to tap more fully into your longing and discontent, what transformational teacher and author Mary Morrissey calls "the two sacred signals from your soul." "If you long for something," she writes, "you want something to shift or change in your life. Feeling discontent shows up in a form of dissatisfaction with your current circumstances."

That is the key distinction: Thus far, these pushes and pulls are happening to you. You are the victim of your external circumstances. If you are to kindle the flames of your longing, you must be willing to admit that these circumstances have opened up a door inside of you—and peer through that door with open eyes and a full heart.

On the other hand, to magnify your dissatisfaction I would encourage you to weigh the costs of delaying your move. I think of my client Kenny, a full-blown hoarder who was running low on savings and needed to sell. He couldn't bring himself to spend the money to empty his densely cluttered apartment. What would have been a few thousand dollars in storage fees to move out the piles of things stacked to the ceiling instead became a $100,000 discount to the final sale price. This classic seller mistake relates more closely to your search than you might recognize. In a way, we're all hoarders, whether we need to get rid of excess junk before we sell or find a home. The difference is that the junk that we refuse to discard is invisible. As an alternative, take an emotional accounting. What are you missing by holding on to the past?

You Can't Hide from the House Hunt

Reality television trivializes this fork in the road between action and inaction. How would it feature the people who haven't overcome their fears and those who fight against uprooting themselves? And how have producers presented the millions of people who never make it beyond their front door, other than by sensationalizing hoarders? The closest producers have come to admitting this is a dilemma is on the long-running show *Love It or List It*, which ended in 2023. What kept homeowners from selling their homes in nearly 60% of the episodes was a professional makeover, complete with gorgeous, albeit temporary, staging furniture. First-time homebuyers have no such opportunity. I would be doing you as grave a disservice as those producers if I sugarcoated that which I have seen so many buyers go through. It isn't all rainbows and unicorns in the real world.

One of the most memorable parables in Michael Singer's *The Untethered Soul* is about a man who builds a house in a light-filled meadow, a house that slowly becomes a fortress. Soon, the man is afraid of everything outside the house's thick protective walls and loses touch with the world. It's meant to exaggerate how our defenses get the better of us. Singer writes, "When you look back at that little house you built, you will wonder why you were ever in there." Finding your dream home is the process of opening the doors, opening the windows, letting in the light, and opening up to new, larger possibilities.

You want to instigate the circumstances such that you can no longer hide from the house hunt, make the truth so obvious that there is no ignoring it. Visualize that early scene in *Harry Potter and the Sorcerer's Stone*, when a single invitation to the wizarding school arrives at 4 Privet Drive. The Dursleys may tear up or burn the letters. They may board up the mail slot, windows, or doorways. But the owls, we soon see, are undaunted. Until his aunt and uncle let Harry hop on the Hogwarts Express, nothing stops the onslaught.

You want your desires to become those owls. So I ask you: What are you holding on to? What is holding you back? What are you hiding from? What are your owls trying to tell you?

The mistake is often in how you have framed the story. It's not that you *have* to move or even that you want to move. You *get* to move. If, like many, you have been living in the frustration of the past or the present, you haven't been spending enough time living in the future. That's where your dreams are, and where you'll find the power to achieve them.

The goal, then, is to start to discover what you would love. Picture yourself opening the front door to your new home. Look around. Feel yourself living every day of your life in the home you have chosen for yourself and your loved ones. Feel the satisfaction of moving forward in the direction you want to take your life. Now pick up a pen. I have created *The Pursuit of Home* Buyer Intake Questionnaire to help you write the first draft of your dream house.

This information is already inside of you. But to bring it out effectively, there is a proper order to how everything is asked. Look at Steve Jobs as an example. He didn't create the original iPod with its dimensions, manufacturing site, or design budget top of mind. He began instead with a big idea: *a thousand songs in your pocket*. It became a rallying cry. That idea ultimately transformed Apple into the juggernaut company we know today. Your big idea is your dream home.

Slow down to let it inspire and infuse you with energy. Let's make this your rallying cry: *Own your move, own your life.*

Only expanded thinking is going to propel you forward. The house hunt needs to be about action, not just motion, right? You build a solid foundation for your home search by laying out what you would really love well ahead of other potentially demoralizing questions. Sure, you should be clear about where you want to live, how much you have to spend, how much you *want* to spend, or the preferred size of your mortgage. Money, though, is more than distracting. Talk about trigger warnings! These are the questions that, asked too quickly, sap your motivation and strength. In the place of action will come the inertia, ambivalence, and fears of negative judgment I touched on earlier.

Go online and see what most other real estate buying guides expect you to prioritize. You will encounter few that attempt to collect more than the most basic data. You might, almost as an afterthought, field a limp catchall question like, *Is there anything we didn't ask you that we should know?* Uncovering the most inspiring information inside of you shouldn't be left to chance, and it shouldn't be at the bottom of a woefully incomplete set of questions.

While it is impossible to have a fully formed idea of what your next home looks like at this point in your search, this questionnaire dares you to tune in to your heart, and then your head. You will be amazed at how much you learn when you go in that order. I will ask you to think about your housing history, and try to put words around what motivated you to rent or buy your current home, and to describe what you have loved about all the homes you have lived in. So be a detective. These choices leave important clues.

Do you have a partner or spouse? Make sure to fill this out separately and then compare your answers. You will find them a great aid to successful communication within your relationship, and with the real estate professionals who will support you. And take heart:

Few couples have started these conversations before they sit down with an agent.

Most important of all, the littlest bit of self-knowledge could tip the scales and get you off that easy chair (which, ironically, isn't so easy to escape from). So get to work! As you will soon see, you will need every ounce of motivation you can find.

The Pursuit of Home
Buyer Intake Questionnaire

Review this questionnaire, and then use the longer version to complete it—online at www.pursueyourhome.com/intake.

Your Big Idea

- Think about when you felt at home somewhere recently. What made it feel that way?
- Put down five words that describe how you feel when you are "home."
- Now, forget the practical. You have no limitations. It's your favorite time of the day, and you're walking around, so grateful for this amazing new place. What would your dream house look like? How many bedrooms? Would it have a shed, a finished basement, a garage, a home office, a gym, a recording studio?
- What finishes and features in other people's homes inspired you? Add anything new to your list.
- Create a home-oriented vision board. What's that, you say? Online home inspiration hub Houzz calls it an ideaboard. Pinterest, a site dedicated to collecting and organizing images of anything, calls it a pinboard. Fashion and design websites call it a lookbook. However and wherever you do your visual discovery, the idea is to put all the images (and words too) that inspire you on one page: your dream kitchen, baths, views, or anything else! For ideas on how to create an

old-school version on posterboard, or a digital vision board on your phone or computer, visit www.pursueyourhome.com/visionboard.

Your Why

- Why do you want to move? Is it something you can put your finger on? Or is it something less tangible?
- If you have a significant other, can you predict their reasons? Are your reasons for moving the same as theirs? ,
- Do you think of these reasons as "good" or "bad"? Do you see your needing to move as an opportunity, or something to complain about?
- When did you realize you were ready for your new home? Did it hit you all at once? If you have a significant other, when did they know? Or did you or they need to be won over?
- Is moving way overdue? What are the financial or emotional costs to waiting?
- On a scale of 1 to 10, how committed are you to moving? What do you need to do before you can be fully committed? If you have a spouse or significant other in this process, what about them? Do you sense any ambivalence?

Your Housing History

- Let's go back and remember your childhood home(s). How many places did you live in? Did you move to different cities? How was one house different from another? How were they the same? Did you share a room?
- Where in your house were you the happiest? What parts of the house did you like best? Describe these details as clearly as you can.
- What did you like about your childhood home(s)? What didn't you like? Be specific. Was it noisy, smelly, or too cramped?
- What other housing experiences did you encounter as a child? Did you go tent or RV camping? Did you go to summer camp, band camp,

bible camp, or some program away from home? Describe what you liked most about them.

- Once you left home, how many places have you lived in? Make a list, along with the dates. Describe what still stands out in those homes. What do they have in common?
- Think about the best place you have ever lived in. The most run-down. The craziest. Describe them in detail, what you loved and what you hated.

Your Current Situation

- Where do you live now?
- What's your marital status? Are you looking to buy a new home with someone else?
- What is your timeline for buying a home? Are you looking to do this in the next three months? Or in the next year?
- Why did you move into your current home? Really dive into why you chose it. Was it the views? The backyard? The kitchen? The nooks and crannies? What else?
- What didn't you realize you would love about it?
- What upgrades have you done that make you love your home even more?
- What is your favorite time of day in your house? What do you do during that time?
- What bothers you, annoys you, or stresses you out about your current house? Is there one thing that you complain about the most? What is it?
- What do others in your home (a child or significant other, perhaps) complain about the most?
- What don't you have right now that would support the things you do in your house, like working from home? That is, what's missing from your current home?
- Now add that one thing. Would it be enough to keep you there?

Your Priorities

- In which towns and neighborhoods are you looking to buy? How did you come to that decision? Are you open to other areas with equally good schools? Gyms? Playgrounds? Houses of worship?
- What are your nice-to-have criteria?
- What is the one thing you absolutely MUST have in your new home? What items are deal-breakers if they are missing? What items could you never live with?
- Are you willing to renovate to add any of these things to (or remove them from) your new home?

The Nuts and Bolts

- Now let's talk about money. How much do you want to spend on your home? How did you come to that number? Are you prioritizing your purchase price or how much you want to spend per month?
- Use this back-of-the-envelope calculation to get a rough idea of what banks think your budget should be. Take your annual income (or your family's). Divide it by twelve to get your monthly income. Banks will look at what's known as a Debt-to-Income (DTI) Ratio to qualify you. This may range from 25% to over 40%. Here's the formula in plain English: Multiply your monthly income number by this percentage number to get your monthly housing budget.

  For instance, an annual income of $60,000 becomes a monthly income of $5,000. If your bank wants to see a DTI of 30%, that translates to a housing budget of $1,500/month ($5,000 x 30%). If this seems like a conservative ratio, don't hold back. Consult a mortgage professional or a real estate agent in your market for other opinions.
- Are you financing? If so, have you gotten preapproved for a mortgage yet? We would recommend you have conversations with mortgage professionals as early as possible.
- If you're financing, how much have you saved for your down payment? After your down payment, what will your post-closing liquid assets be?

- You'll want to look at all of your assets (cash, stocks, bonds, retirement accounts) and liabilities (your debts), and your income, in one place. Fill in the blanks on the balance sheet in the appendix or online (www .pursueyourhome.com/balancesheet will add up your assets auto- matically!) to get a basic look. Don't worry about being accurate to the penny, though there are many other resources that will be more com- prehensive if you feel this to be necessary, and your mortgage lender will require this later anyway. What's most important at present is to see your finances in black and white.

   IMPORTANT: Take a few minutes to think about (then input) any other resources you have. For example, will your family or friends help you with your down payment?

- Depending on mortgage rates, down payment requirements, and the different lending programs and loan products available when you're reading this, you'll have a better sense of the mortgage you can take. We have also provided a mortgage calculator on our website for you to use (www.pursueyourhome.com/mortgagecalculator).

Before We Move On

Notice how the Nuts and Bolts made you feel. Are you distracted, annoyed, or even depressed now? Let's fix that:

- Review your Why—your reasons for moving—and remind yourself of the emotional costs of staying where you are.
- Reread all the things that you would love in your new home.
- Take another long look at that vision board. Plan to look at it as often as you can, perhaps every morning during your home search.

And One More Thing

To whom do you turn for guidance? Whose advice do you value? Who are your personal and professional mentors? Who listens without judgment and helps you make important decisions? Not just that, but who are those people that lift you up? Who celebrates your successes with you? How wonderful is it to have these people in your life? My advice is to call them often. Share that you are starting to look for a new home, if you haven't already. Let them know that you might need their help when things get weird.

As to those people in your life who judge you, or whom you feel hold you back in any way from making big moves—you know who they are. They don't need to be along for this ride, do they? At the very least, they don't have to ride shotgun.

Feeling good again? Great! Let's do this!

CHAPTER 3

Listings Aren't Enough

Choosing the Right Real Estate Agent for You

*"We celebrate Independence Day; we don't
celebrate We Desperately Rely on Others
Day . . . Our great American mythology tends to
celebrate separate achievement and separateness,
when in fact nobody does anything alone."*
—Barbara Kingsolver

Crossing the Threshold

Slim Aarons's drool-worthy 1960s photographs were the real estate daydreams of yesteryear, iconic images of *Mad Men*–era poolside gatherings, the original behind-the-scenes images of gorgeous people doing clandestine luxury activities. Now you can pan around your neighbor's home anytime you like, often in 3D, anywhere you have a screen. Add in a nearly endless stream of infinity pools, curated interior design ideas, and luxury tours on Instagram, TikTok, and Houzz, to name a few, and you get what many call real estate porn. This is the tech-enabled world in which you will start your home search in earnest. Soon enough, you will also find your way to Zillow.

Zillow, founded in 2006, is the starting line for most would-be buyers, and the most trafficked real estate website in America. It's a whirlwind of manicured lawns, drone shots, kitchens, baths, and bedrooms. Best of all, this smorgasbord is free to house-curious consumers like you. *Saturday Night Live* once poked fun at scrolling these websites as a replacement for sex when you reach your 30s. In its place are fantasies about doing renovations and houses that you know you'll never buy, what was recently called "Zillow Therapy."

However, if you are serious about buying, these options can only stand in for touring homes in person for so long. Eventually, you will want to touch and feel and viscerally experience them. The most common transition from the virtual to the real world will take you through open houses. Drive through any neighborhood on a weekend, and the temporary placards in the shape of an arrow will point you to properties you can visit without an appointment.

It's one thing to look carefully at why you want to make this big move. It's another to use a vision board to better see the facade in your mind's eye. As you walk through an actual front door, though, your compass may already be spinning out of control. The conversations with the listing agents at open houses are not what you expected. Nor do you like walking around someone else's home alongside complete strangers. The spiritual teacher Richard Alpert, more commonly known as Ram Dass, is purported to have said, "If you think you are enlightened, go and spend a week with your family." I'll put my twist on this. If you think you are ready to buy a home, go spend a day at open houses.

The open house is a liminal space, from the Latin word *limen*, meaning "threshold." You've crossed a physical boundary from the world you know into a new domain teeming with new possibilities. Think about other liminal spaces, such as bars, airports, art galleries, hotels, and museums, and the welcoming smiles from the bartender, flight attendant, or concierge. They offer the promise of sanctuary, with an assist from alcohol, a cart of snacks, or a basket of apples in a scent-infused lobby. That is just enough to melt away your fear and allow your curiosity to emerge.

In an open house, agents might bake cookies, but their aroma won't always keep you from tensing up. I have witnessed hundreds of buyers hiding their earnest desire for a new home behind crossed arms, scrunched-up faces, and barrages of information-gathering questions. The house dissolves into a frightening, overwhelming morass of mortgage rates, inspections, negotiations, bidding wars, and endless minutiae. You may be experiencing your first anxiety and uncertainty in your search. Or perhaps you are flashing back to some awful real estate foray long ago or a recent appointment with a salesperson you didn't like who wouldn't stop talking and didn't understand that you just needed some silence in which to look around.

In many ways, the house hunt begins like any New Year's resolution, designed with initial anticipation and eventually eroded by demotivation. Like wanting to get in shape, signing up for a gym membership only gets you so far. Then the fantasy hits reality. Your search has been in beta testing. And boy are there a lot of bugs. How long before you slump back onto the couch in temporary, or permanent, defeat?

Homes.com, a competitor to Zillow, proudly advertises that "We've done your homework." Alas, they haven't. Listings are not enough. How could they be? What's missing from this promise is a partnership to keep you inspired—and a way to find it. Because you certainly cannot overcome inertia, fears of negative judgment, or ambivalence alone. This chapter is about solving the not-so-little problem of finding the right partner.

🏠 🏠 🏠

Back to the hero's journey for a moment. Think of the main characters of every beloved epic. They, too, began as fearful and doubtful initiates in a haze of ambivalence and dissatisfaction.

Then young King Arthur gets Merlin. Frodo and his ring-fellows greet Gandalf in the Shire. Cinderella's Fairy Godmother floats in to rescue her. Luke Skywalker finds out that old man Ben, whom he had once dismissed as a kook, is the great Jedi Knight Obi-Wan Kenobi. These mystical mentors provide the essential spark and confidence for each hero to begin their harrowing adventures in earnest. The big difference here is that you must seek out your guide. We are, of course, talking about finding a real estate agent to work with.

A recent study showed that more than 90% of consumers employed real estate agents in their transactions. So, this isn't an unusual mission by any stretch. But how should you go about finding an agent *effectively*?

A 2023 NAR report tracked the most typical methods first-time buyers used to do so. The results: referral (40%), property inquiry (7%), online search (7%), other (46%). That means 60% of buyers hired an agent without a referral. How they make their decisions is instructive. That is, it points to what you should not do. Chew on this: 71% of buyers interviewed only one agent. You can understand, then, why Zillow earns more than a billion dollars a year from its variety of agent advertising platforms. They are powerful weapons to woo a massive group of unrepresented buyers who may spend longer planning their vacations than researching whom they hire. Considering an agent's expertise, or lack thereof, will shape the outcome of their lives, that is remarkably undiscerning behavior. If you can't sympathize with this snap decision, however, you will eventually. Even the greenest sales agent you meet can't botch a pitch like this. All they have to do is tap in to your enticing dream. And all you have to do is get swept up in it.

Economists might also point out that the long-standing business model—where sellers, not buyers, paid buyer agents—incentivizes buyers to make hasty hiring decisions. Even without an economics degree, you can see how buyers might not weigh their options as carefully when they don't perceive a direct cost. Financial incentives aside, few homebuyers fully assess the role a buyer agent plays beyond logistical and transactional expertise. They don't value the relationship itself.

🏠 🏠 🏠

Buyers feel that agents don't really care about them either. Even renters tread carefully. They are both right to do so. How do I know? I was a leasing agent once, and I was no saint. I once doctored credit reports with a pair of scissors, whiteout, and a copy machine. I regularly jimmied open door locks with credit cards. I thought long and hard about bribing building superintendents, but could never bring myself to do it. It was a hustle, only one step above a game of three-card monte in Times Square's seedier days.

The air was only moderately more breathable as I began working with buyers and sellers. So many agents lied to my face that "get it in writing" became my mantra. Who can't name at least one award-winning agent caricature from the array of grifters, swindlers, and charlatans who have graced the silver screen? From the desperation of Annette Bening's character in *American Beauty*, to the star-studded cast of slimy salesmen in David Mamet's *Glengarry Glen Ross*, to a scathing indictment of the entire industry in *The Big Short*, you could rightly say that real estate professionals are held in lower esteem than politicians and ambulance chasers. Did bluffing on behalf of my clients sometimes blur into outright lying? You bet it did. One might just call that salesmanship. But there is a line, and I am not proud of how often I crossed it myself—before I turned away from the dark side some years ago.

I interviewed Drs. Frank and Laurie Zelinger, licensed therapists in Long Island and bestselling authors, about the couples they treat and the conversations they have behind closed doors about real estate. What are their clients telling them about their experiences with agents?

"I hear more criticism," Frank said. "Clients have told me, 'I wish my broker would have shown this to me earlier,' or 'How come he didn't show me this?' Or, 'It's not remotely what I want.' 'Just make the deal' is how they are describing agents. . . . The most common thing I hear is, 'Oh yeah, she sold my friend's house.' [That's] not the intimacy of relationship."

Laurie continued. "People aren't talking [to their agent] about their 'big why.' They are afraid to frame it in this way, to reveal their dreams, because it reflects poorly on them if they can't [make them a reality]."

It's all right there: your natural fear and mistrust. This is a huge thing! Of course it's scary! Therefore, an agent's chief role—and yours—should be to face down and eliminate these foes. Hall Willkie, the longtime president of New York City–based Brown Harris Stevens, put it to me this way when I was starting out: "You're not in the real estate business. You're in the relationship business."

The old joke is that agents are therapists. And yes, brokerage firms usually pay lip service to this idea that agents are here for more than facilitating a sale in their ads and on their websites. What are most real estate companies and their agents really doing about it, though? Not very much.

Jimmy Burgess, the CEO for Berkshire Hathaway HomeServices Beach Properties of Florida, mapped out why he thought real estate brokers are and will always remain important. His top reasons were: (1) experience, (2) key local knowledge, (3) network of local resources, (4) valuation expertise, (5) negotiation skills, (6) marketing skills, and (7) legal navigation through the process. Why aren't relationships on this list?

I discussed this with John Leonardi, the CEO of the Buffalo Niagara Association of Realtors®, who oversees 3,700 member agents with an average deal size of $280,000. The most successful agents in his region will do more than 200 sales a year. That kind of volume requires a well-oiled machine. Leonardi told me that one of his members had even mapped out 151 steps to the buying process. When I asked him where "getting to know the buyers" fit onto that map, however, he noticed that it didn't.

The top 20 nationally ranked teams doubled that region's superstars in their number of sales. A few so-called "mega teams" cranked out more than five times that number, according to RealTrends, an organization that tracks transactions and publishes them to much end-of-year fanfare. However, I have never seen a real estate poll try to measure the strength of an agent–buyer relationship, nor how that strength translates into doing more business for these teams. And even if these same publications were to compile a star agent's meetings, phone calls, texts, or emails as a proxy for how they build relationships with their clients, would the industry really care? It's far less marketable than the output: commission and, ultimately, income.

Coaches First, Agents Second

It is due to this transaction-oriented agent mindset that buyers' resentment and anger have festered. You have a right to be angry if an agent puts their success before yours. You want an agent who has a relationship-oriented mindset. And your introductory conversation with them should never start with an information exchange about your budget, your income, or your checklist. If it does, I guarantee that something will feel off. They should already know the basics of real estate, but those are just the table stakes. An agent's overarching work is to build a relationship with you and serve as your coach. The dynamic can feel very different, and more positive, when the personal relationship gets the weight it deserves.

A coach imbues you with the confidence that you are going to get better. Then he pushes you to dig within and achieve something that is bigger than yourself. Think of the small-town Indiana basketball squad in the movie *Hoosiers*. By using a different communication style with each player, Gene Hackman's character, Norman Dale, brings out the best in all of them, and leads the team to a state championship.

There's a reason that millions tuned in to an American television series about a goofy Midwestern soccer coach named Ted Lasso. We still long for people like that in our lives. Author Jon Acuff put it well in his book *Finish*: "We don't ever age out of needing someone to believe in us." The only reason I have my real estate career at all is because my stepmother suggested I get my license. She saw something in me I didn't see in myself.

I also remember that I once worried more about paying my bills than being of service to my clients—not exactly the collaborative spirit you want from your agent. No one told me that real estate was a team sport, nor how much more value I could bring by putting on the coach's hat before anything else. Your agent's priority should be the satisfaction of helping you win. That selflessness is crucial to the process of clearing away your early doubts and fears. As we will establish, there's a lot happening within you and all around you that's not obvious at first glance.

The Magnetic Method

The Earth features a magnetic field that surrounds us. You only need a compass to see how it exerts its invisible force on the world. This notion of the power of what we cannot see directing us and guiding us forward informs everything I do with my team and my clients. It led me to call our system of helping buyers and sellers The Magnetic Method.

At its core, our system aims to pare away, and repel, everything that isn't your dream home. It is our responsibility to reshape that conference room, Zoom screen, coffee shop, or open house into a judgment-free zone where you can begin to turn on the energetic pull of your ever-larger dreams. We aim to convert your confusion, paralysis, or stuck-ness into *action*. Whatever baggage you bring with you, and however much you've stuffed in there, we want you to feel comfortable to unpack it with us or get rid of it altogether.

Now and then my clients share why they introduced me to their friends who are buying or selling. One person said, "I told my friend that I'm connecting you because you're not a jackass." Another soon-to-be client said she was intrigued by her friend's description of me, which to her sounded like an oxymoron: I was, apparently, a "lovely broker." She didn't think that kind of real estate professional existed! I began to see what made me stand out from other real estate agents. I bring this up now because it describes the kind of agent that might best serve you: someone who cares about your success, and whose care shines through everything they do. All of this comes together in The Magnetic Method, designed to draw you to your home, as if you were simply one magnet finding another nearby. Its four steps are four A's: Activate, Align, Amplify, and Attract. Deploying it is like having a magic lodestone to guide you home.

STEP ONE: ACTIVATE

Your agent needs to get to know you before you can be magnetized. Forget your paperwork, your budget, or your timeline for a while. Who are you as a person? What are you up to in the world? Where would you love to live? What could that home look like? We learn where you're coming from so we can dream together with you. What you say and what you don't say are equally important. This is the openhearted understanding and much-needed break from the action you didn't know you were looking for.

This discovery process may start as a formal meeting, but it takes more than an hour in a conference room for you to let down your guard. I am thinking about when my team and I were struggling recently with new buyers Jane and Brian. Based on her snippy emails, I thought Jane was going to fire us. I asked her to get on a phone call.

Together, we uncrated her unspoken assumptions. She had expected that we would be in touch daily, even if just to say that there were no new properties available. From her perspective, how could we add value otherwise? I told her we were glad to add that short email to our to-do list—a minor shift that worked wonders in calming her down and gaining her trust.

The Magnetic Method

The Easiest Way to Find Your Home

Activate — Create a Compelling and Motivating First Draft of the Vision of Your Home

Align — Gain Clarity Around Your True Likes and Dislikes

Amplify — Broadcast Your Crystal-Clear Vision Across All Our Channels to Generate a Powerful Magnetic Pull

Attract — Make Your Own Market, and Let Your Home Find You

These are not typical conversations, mind you. So how did I pull it off? Because I had told her, in our intake meeting, what we tell all our clients: "Tell us if and when things aren't going well." I don't take that lightly, because it requires a willingness to take any feedback and still not be defensive—no matter how harsh the criticism. What it does, though, is provide clients like this permission to speak their minds.

Feeling that someone "gets you" is important. Especially so when you want out of your cramped one-bedroom apartment, when not having a bigger home is the block between you and your husband having a second child. Our job is to make room for anything that needs to be said. Fred Rogers, known better as Mister Rogers, put it brilliantly to his television audience years ago: "Anything mentionable is manageable." Implementing that philosophy goes a long way toward achieving your real estate goals.

Chapter 2's Buyer Intake Questionnaire was intended to help you create the enticing first draft of your vision of a dream home on your own. Adding a good agent into the mix should make this learning period more comprehensive.

STEP TWO: ALIGN

Helping your agent understand you is, by definition, a trust-building exercise. This facet of The Magnetic Method is where the rubber meets the road, and when the first draft of your vision will be tested. What might this relationship with your agent look like? It will vary, but I know it inhabits a safe enough space, in a manner of speaking, where you can be both comfortable and uncomfortable, where you begin to repel what you don't like, and discover what you do. Your agent's experience, perspective, and confidence must be sufficient to prod, poke, and provoke your preconceived notions and long-held checklists in a thoughtful, caring way.

As you Align your magnetic fields inside your magnet—and align your vision with those important partners involved—you often discover that you only need certain information, far less than you imagined, to proceed in earnest. Alan and his wife, Blair, are a good example. Alan had been in limbo, believing that by waiting to lock in a long-term position with his hospital he would also remove the unknowns about the location and budget for their search. An unskilled agent might have played along. However, our further discussions uncovered that he already knew more or less what his salary would be, and that they wanted to stay in Manhattan rather than move to the suburbs. So what was missing? Only one data point: Would he have enough of a budget and income to afford what he wanted in the city, or not? "I hadn't done the work, because maybe I was afraid of the answer," Alan later revealed. It was as if he were avoiding going to the doctor, for fear of a diagnosis of not-enough-money-itis.

Alan needed someone to give it to him straight. Fortunately, the market offered them a clean bill of financial health, so to speak, and a green light to live in the city. With a less experienced agent, however, Alan and Blair may have waited too long, missed a lull in the market, and may have been forced to look elsewhere. Aligning started the magnetizing process far earlier than they had anticipated.

STEP THREE: AMPLIFY

After you Activate and Align your magnet, you and your agent Amplify its strength by further refining your vision, so it generates an ever-stronger pull. He or she should be suggesting out-of-the-box listings, or proposing offbeat solutions, anything to keep you on your toes and out of your head. How do you know it's working? Soon enough, the market, and not your agent, will begin to push back with all sorts of challenging situations. Never fear! Magnets get stronger in the cold. Your agent will also help boost your property magnet's signal with continued coaching and inspiration.

The by-product of this Amplification is a growing intuition you'll want to rely upon more and more. Once you open up a little bit, it will start nudging you. You will have to listen more carefully and intently than you ever have before. Don't dismiss or discount any random or spontaneous ideas that start to appear, and which may not make logical sense to either of you. They often prove unbelievably helpful.

STEP FOUR: ATTRACT

More than a plan of attack or a strategy, we are guided by a *belief* that your home is possible. It becomes an expectation and a matter of faith that it will happen, even as that faith is pushed to the brink. Along the way, a clear image of your future house comes into focus, until you know exactly what your home should be and it is drawn into your life. We are here to guide you until that home appears, until it is a reality. The Magnetic Method and its four A's are a formula for success, then, that looks like this:

ACTIVATE + ALIGN + AMPLIFY = ATTRACT

🏠 🏠 🏠

Once upon a time, a magnet could only be created with the help of a preexisting one. That remains true in real estate, except in this case the other property magnet is your agent. And there will always be one breakthrough in a healthy buyer–agent working relationship when your agent's magnetic power and value becomes clear and helps bring your dream to fruition. I don't know when that moment will be, but I know it will happen. This is the promise of The Magnetic Method. This is my promise to you.

House Hunter, Know Thyself

Something akin to The Magnetic Method is what I hope every buyer agent might offer his or her clients. However, there's still only so much your agent can do. Every coach is on the sidelines—and you are on the court. You have to take all the shots. So it's time to hold up your end of the bargain.

Magicians, wizards, and fairy godmothers are only symbols for the guides of your hero's journey, not the reality. Agents cannot read minds, any more than your spouse can. So you need to be able to effectively communicate with your agent. How do you do that? By being in better communication with yourself.

You have already made a long checklist of all the things you want in your new house. We could call these the answers to the *what* questions: location, bedroom count, and the like. You also took a shot at dreaming big and answering the less-measurable questions: Why do you want to move? What are you moving away from? What are you moving toward?

In the previous chapter, you also compiled a list of your financial resources. But there are other resources we have only hinted at so far—the resources inside of you. Here, and in subsequent chapters, you will need to do an accounting of who you are, not just what you have or how you feel. I offer you a new group of questions that are not directly related to what's driving your purchase, or to any particular properties, but to you and your personality. You, too, may persist in thinking of this as a transaction. But you can't escape your personality when you start looking for a home.

Again, this partnership between you and your agent requires effective communication. So we must learn how your personality operates. For instance, how do you work with other people? What are your go-to mental frameworks for making decisions? How do you react under pressure? How honest do you like people to be with you? How sensitive are you to bad news? How do you react when you don't get what you want?

How you filter information anywhere is how you will filter information in your home search. You might want every data point. Or you may get lost in dreaming about the idea of your house. Details may not be your thing. You may say, "I only need a high-level summary to make these kinds of decisions." Alternatively, the safety of a house might be at the top of your priority list. In line with this, you may be more inclined to put everyone else's needs in front of your own. Alternatively, the future of the neighborhood and its appreciation potential may strike you as far more important.

Author Gary Chapman wrote about love languages. You have a *house language* too. This is your unique communication style that, if ignored by your agent, will leave you displeased and distracted. You'll feel like no one is listening to you. You will feel like your needs aren't being met. And you could miss great properties just because an agent's tone of voice or manner of communication trips your defenses. The choice to work with any professional can't be made in a vacuum, or from a résumé. It should be made in the context of how they work in relation to you.

But we're getting ahead of ourselves. There are many more components to your personality that we should identify now, rather than later. These relate to disclosure, trust, and negotiation. Do you keep your desires close to the vest? Would constant questions from your agent strike you as nosy or prying? Do you start new relationships from a place of trust or mistrust?

How do you negotiate? You may have been raised to believe that every negotiation cranks out a winner and a loser, and to lose a negotiation is to be a sucker. You may rather die than pay retail. Or negotiating may be far from your cultural norm.

I don't expect you to overcome your dispositions, nor should your agent. But you do need to be aware of them. This is an invitation to know more about yourself, and learn what you need to thrive amid unexpected and high-stress encounters.

There are a lot of general personality assessments, such as the Myers-Briggs personality test that divides people along the lines of introversion vs. extroversion, sensing vs. intuition, thinking vs. feeling, or judging vs. perceiving. I have never seen these tools applied to real estate, at least not in a way that helps you take action toward your goals.

Therefore, I created a new tool, *The Pursuit of Home* Buyer Personality Profile Assessment.† It was inspired by and distilled from many other much longer quizzes, and tailored for your home search. After you answer just 10 painless questions, you will have your Buyer Personality Profile—along with a template for effective communication. Your friends, family, and real estate professionals will thank you. You might learn something too.

Your Buyer Personality Profile Assessment

Get ready to take your *Buyer Personality Profile Assessment*. It should take you less than five minutes to complete. IMPORTANT: There are no right answers! So don't overthink your answers to each question. Your instinctual reaction is best. Circle your answers: Strongly Agree, Agree, Undecided, Disagree, or Strongly Disagree.

1. In choosing a home, it is most important that it feels welcoming and comfortable for my family and friends.

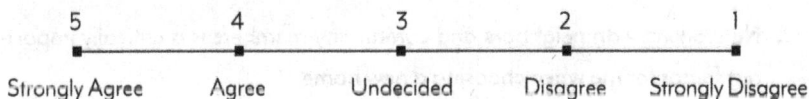

5	4	3	2	1
Strongly Agree	Agree	Undecided	Disagree	Strongly Disagree

2. I am most drawn to homes with unique, innovative features or design elements that stand out from the typical property.

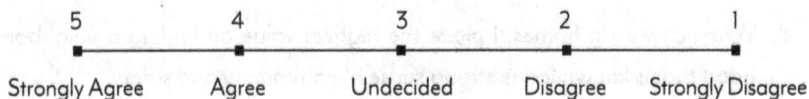

5	4	3	2	1
Strongly Agree	Agree	Undecided	Disagree	Strongly Disagree

---

† To complete this online, go to www.pursueyourhome.com/assessment.

3. It is very important to discuss home options with family, friends, and real estate agents to get diverse perspectives before making a decision.

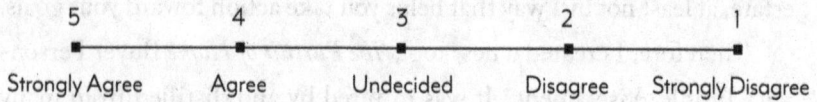

5	4	3	2	1
Strongly Agree	Agree	Undecided	Disagree	Strongly Disagree

4. I am able to easily see the potential for a home to be transformed or renovated even if its current condition is poor.

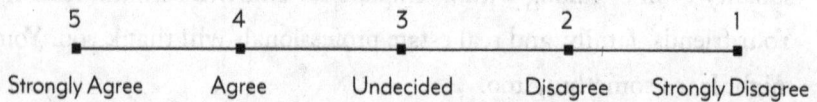

5	4	3	2	1
Strongly Agree	Agree	Undecided	Disagree	Strongly Disagree

5. I prioritize and strongly value a practical and functional layout in a home, with an emphasis on reliability and ease of maintenance.

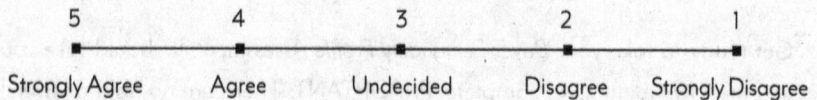

5	4	3	2	1
Strongly Agree	Agree	Undecided	Disagree	Strongly Disagree

6. I would strongly prefer an emerging neighborhood or a fixer-upper with great potential if it meant the best return on my real estate investment.

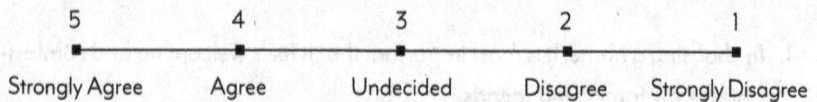

5	4	3	2	1
Strongly Agree	Agree	Undecided	Disagree	Strongly Disagree

7. Networking with neighbors and community members is a critically important factor for me when choosing a new home.

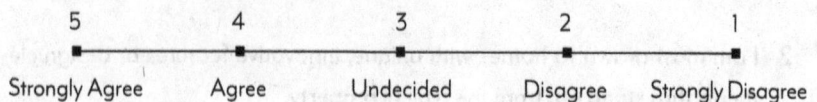

5	4	3	2	1
Strongly Agree	Agree	Undecided	Disagree	Strongly Disagree

8. When assessing homes, I place the highest value on finding a neighborhood that is known for its strong sense of community and safety.

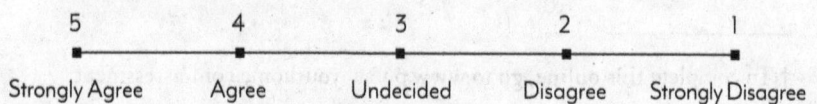

5	4	3	2	1
Strongly Agree	Agree	Undecided	Disagree	Strongly Disagree

9. I am compelled to buy a home in a well-established area that has a proven track record of home sales.

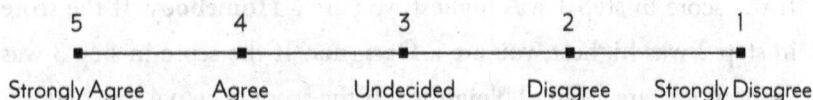

5	4	3	2	1
Strongly Agree	Agree	Undecided	Disagree	Strongly Disagree

10. More than anything, I believe purchasing a home is a strategic investment, first evaluating factors like market trends and appreciation upside.

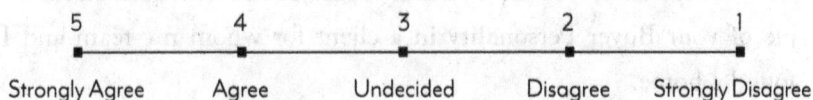

5	4	3	2	1
Strongly Agree	Agree	Undecided	Disagree	Strongly Disagree

Scoring Your Assessment in Six Steps

Step 1: Add together the scores for questions 1 and 8.

Step 2: Add together the scores for questions 2 and 4.

Step 3: Add together the scores for questions 3 and 7.

Step 4: Add together the scores for questions 5 and 9.

Step 5: Add together the scores for questions 6 and 10.

Step 6: Look for any answer where you marked "strongly disagree," then follow the directions. If you didn't answer "strongly disagree," skip the directions below:

- For question 1, add one point to your score in step 5.
- For question 2, add one point to your score in step 4.
- For question 3, add one point to your score in step 2.
- For question 4, add one point to your score in step 4.
- For question 5, add one point to your score in step 2.
- For question 6, add one point to your score in step 1.
- For question 7, add one point to your score in step 5.
- For question 8, add one point to your score in step 3.
- For question 9, add one point to your score in step 5.
- For question 10, add one point to your score in step 1.

The Five Buyer Personality Types

If the score in step 1 was highest, you are a **Homebody**. If the score in step 2 was highest, you are a **Designer**. If the score in step 3 was highest, you are a **Good Neighbor**. If the score in step 4 was highest, you are a **Meter Reader**. If the score in step 5 was highest, you are a **House Manager**.

I'll explain how each personality operates and then offer an example of your Buyer Personality in a client for whom my team and I found a home.

The Homebody

Homebodies are always working to create a nurturing and welcoming home. This is the quietest and most sensitive Buyer Personality. Resistant to change, and occasionally passive-aggressive, this buyer type will always prioritize the "happy home" rather than its details.

In the context of the house hunt, they are seeking more personal connection and support than other Buyer Personalities. They are also fiercely loyal. Even in this setting, they constantly worry about everyone else's feelings more than their own. For example, they would never dare move forward with a purchase without their children seeing a property. When it comes to choosing an agent, they give the most weight to their closest friends' recommendations. NOTE: This could cause conflict later if their friends haven't referred them to a high-quality agent. But I digress.

If you are a Homebody, you are in a big club. Almost half of homebuyers are Homebodies. This may also be a big reason why all homeowners only move every nine years on average. Homebodies are resistant to changing the status quo.

♠ ♠ ♠

Arden and Seth are a perfect example of Homebodies. They had bought their home in the suburbs for all of the practical reasons: good public schools, proximity to Seth's hospital work, an easier life. They were the kind of parents who sacrificed to give their children every advantage. The only thing that would move them was going to be a big change, such as a job relocation, or eventually wanting to be closer to their kids years after they flew the nest.

This big change came sooner than they expected when Seth's medical group was sold. With some extra money in their pocket, they expanded their thinking on what taking care of their family looked like. It wasn't a country house that they wanted for weekend getaways. That felt too similar to the house they already owned.

They could see more plainly, more purely, what was most import-ant to them and what would make their kids happier, which would in turn make them happier. It was having a second home in Manhattan near their old friends, and somewhere that would force the family to spend more time together. It was about strengthening their relation-ships rather than stretching their legs, since anything was going to be smaller than their large suburban house.

For a family of four, they had assumed they would find a two-bedroom apartment to buy. We even bid on a couple. But their Home-body personalities prevailed; they sought out closer quarters and instead zeroed in on a large one-bedroom apartment I heard about before it hit the market. Their friends took part in the decision. Their children were looking forward to crashing on pullout couches in the living room. The negotiation took on this unusually joyous tone, all the way to the closing table.

Those drives back and forth from nearby suburban Westchester have also taken on new meaning. Arden said, "I was kind of down on the suburbs before we got our place in the city. After getting the place in the city, I love the city and being there, but I also love coming back to the suburbs. It's like I can appreciate both so much more."

The Designer

Conversely, Designers are always future-oriented, and enticed by special and innovative homes. This may include gadgets or, on the other end of the spectrum, unique architectural features. They are thinking outside the four walls. They can conceptualize a home from a floor plan. Every property is a blank canvas with endless possibilities. They are excited about customizing a home to match their unique vision and exceptional taste. They are the impulse buyers, and sometimes change their minds just as quickly.

Designers are exceedingly rare but essential in the real estate ecosystem. They are often the people who become interior decorators, architects, and even real estate agents. If you are a Designer, don't be confused when others cannot peer through the crumbling plaster and conceive of a finished product as you do. Because it can be very frustrating.

🏠 🏠 🏠

I met Patty at the open house of our exclusive listing that, in the words of my contractor, was in "the worst condition I've ever seen." Strong words for someone whose work consists of updating unrenovated properties. True to her Designer personality, Patty loved the possibilities of what she could create there. It would give her an extra bedroom and much more living space than where she currently lived.

My colleague Jonathan and I sat down with her to map out what a timeline might look like to buy the apartment and have us sell hers. She was a therapist, but thought about becoming a real estate agent as her retirement neared. She had either totally revamped or built from the ground up every home she had ever owned, including properties in the Hamptons and elsewhere. Something held Patty back from this ambitious renovation, though nothing else gave her enough room for her creativity, certainly not the newly constructed buildings she had us show her nearby.

That something was a possibility Patty had mulled over, but dismissed before we met her: buying her neighbor's apartment. She had gotten hung up on the potential restrictions a bank might give her on borrowing for the purchase, given that it wasn't yet officially connected to hers. There was a risk that a bank underwriter would consider this adjacent unit an investment property and charge her a hefty premium on her mortgage rate as a result.

We studied the situation further and gave her a strategy for mitigating that risk. The property had been on the market for six months with no takers. Why not negotiate a little more aggressively? If her lender gave her any grief, a lower price would more than make up for the higher borrowing rate. If not, she'd be way ahead. And once she combined the units, she would be able to refinance them, anyway, as a single property. Before you dismiss apartment combinations as nothing more than a strange concept unique to city living, homeowners everywhere buy homes that need renovation. Financing that purchase before the work begins, paying for that work out of pocket, and pulling out renovation costs in a refinance afterward may function very much the same way.

And, like Patty, you would only endure the pain of renovating if it were financially appealing. Hers was a vastly better deal than the other properties we had visited. She saved a small fortune by avoiding the costs of selling, and her building sold her a portion of hallway space in front of her apartment that made the finished space connect even more seamlessly. After her work was done and everything was paid for, the combined units are worth about half a million dollars more than her investment.

Much like combining apartments, it takes the same creative mind to envision the final product in an unrenovated house. Having a Designer's vision serves you well either way.

The Good Neighbor

Good Neighbors enjoy the house hunt even more than Designers. Extroverted, social, and relationship-oriented, they highly value the people and connections they'll make in their new neighborhood. For them, it is not just about finding a house, but a community where they can be actively involved.

Good Neighbors may only jump into the market when other people they trust—not agents—either advise them to do so or are buying themselves. Social proof and consensus building are key. Both charismatic and good at networking, they are the people who, whatever you need with your renovation, say, "I know just who you need to call!"

Good Neighbors are less concerned about details and will butt heads with those who are. Never fear, though. I still treasure a Good Neighbor's uncommon qualities. Only about one in ten buyers are Good Neighbors.

🛎 🛎 🛎

Do you think you have to act like a jerk when you're in the scrum of a negotiation for a home purchase? That idea would have been anathema to Daria, who embodied all the characteristics of a Good Neighbor when she bought her home. Daria makes friends wherever she goes. To her, the big city is nothing but a series of small villages put together. And she's the mayor of them all. Why would it make sense to mistreat your friends and "constituents"? This premise didn't change one bit when she found her new home. In fact, her relationships were the primary reason her complicated purchase and sale came together. Not only did she have the opportunity to buy her neighbor's apartment two floors up, but when it was over, she was looking forward to living near the new owners of her old apartment too. It's the kind of move that only a Good Neighbor would make.

The people from whom she was buying the new apartment were her good friends who loved the idea of selling to her. Importantly, they made an up-front agreement that their personal relationship would always take priority over potentially uncomfortable money conversations. It was that intention that probably took the edge off those conversations, knowing they could iron them out through thoughtful communication.

Daria has enough self-awareness to understand how she operates. "I'm a very relational person. It's the thing that anchors me in life. I can't imagine embarking on this . . . with people that I don't know. My life is filled with an intricate web of significant relationships. That's how my life works." Anyone could have predicted, too, that Daria and I were also good friends before I became her agent.

We quickly found a buyer for her old apartment, but I was involved in the most discombobulating part of the process for Daria—when she had no relationships to rely upon. Daria's biggest sources of stress were those areas of the transaction. While her mortgage came through another personal connection, the bank's underwriters were anonymous, and therefore impervious to her interpersonal strengths. Along those lines, Daria shared further frustration. "The biggest [relationship] deficit was with the people buying the apartment," she said. "I was like, 'Can I just have their cell phone numbers?'" She desperately wanted, and felt compelled, really, to deepen that relationship too. Does this sound like any negotiation you've ever had? If so, you might be a Good Neighbor.

The Meter Reader

Far from the warmth of the Good Neighbor, Meter Readers are practical, cautious, logical, and methodical. They prize information, accuracy, and thorough analysis. They seek a secure and dependable home. Meter Readers are the ones who ensure everything is in order, from the home's structural integrity to the neighborhood's safety. Grounded and detail-oriented, they also center themselves around practical layouts and building long-term equity. They must ensure the home has a solid foundation, both literally and figuratively.

They want a framework and a system in place before making a decision to purchase. Therefore, they ask the tough questions. They have spreadsheets. They aren't sentimental like Homebodies either. They know there is a "right decision" to be made, one that other people's feelings sometimes obscure. If they had a factory setting, it would be set to "no." Skeptical by nature, they need facts to build trust.

These are the buyers who measure their furniture to make sure it will fit. These buyers have no FOMO (fear of missing out), but they certainly fear making a mistake. If you are a Meter Reader, you may take longer to purchase than other Buyer Personality types. But you're not alone. Nearly one in three buyers are Meter Readers.

🏠 🏠 🏠

I stay in contact with my former clients, but the Meter Readers I know do not always return my calls until they have critical real estate information to gather. Until then, they're too busy immersed in other areas of their life. One afternoon, Debbie called me, panicked. "Scott, can we sit down tomorrow? I have a decision to make." We met at a Midtown fast casual spot for lunch. She had come a long way from being the new New Yorker fresh out of business school. Over salads, we caught up on her life, her career, and, as we had always bonded over our mutual love of long-distance running, her latest marathon.

"Scott, I want to buy either in the Hamptons or in the city. I can't do both," she said. She had gotten to know the area "out east," slang for the easternmost end of Suffolk County that includes both the North and South Forks of Long Island. She had rented houses over the years during the bustling summer months, during which she saw friends, went to the beach occasionally, and ran along the quiet, picturesque roads dotted with hedges, farmland, nature preserves, and ocean vistas. Choosing between the Hamptons and Manhattan should have been fun, but Debbie treated the decision as if it were a business school case study. This is typical of Meter Readers, who crave detailed information, efficiency, and thorough market analysis in every real estate decision. It was only troubling her because she had become stuck in analysis paralysis.

Knowing that, I gently cut her off when she pulled out a list of pros and cons. I asked her, "What would you love in your home?"

Before she could catch herself, she blurted, "I want to be able to go out to the Hamptons anytime and hang out with friends." Five seconds earlier, Debbie didn't have this answer. Then she heard it coming from her own mouth. She thought she needed more practical and financial real estate expertise. What she needed was motivation and a little direction. As soon as she spoke, she had made her real estate decision. Encouragement had bridged the gap between her left brain and her right brain.

It didn't hurt that during her search, it was a buyer's market in the Hamptons. A few months later, with the help of my talented colleague, Debbie was the proud owner of one of the only log cabins in the entire area, ready for her summer adventures. When COVID-19 descended on the city, she moved there full-time and gave up her city rental altogether. As I write this, she still hasn't moved back.

The House Manager

House Managers are the rarest Buyer Personality—and the most assertive, goal-oriented, and results-driven. They look for homes that are not just dwellings, but smart investments as well. They are somewhat ahead of the curve, spotting trends and potential in the housing market. Forward-thinking and decisive, House Managers are not afraid to explore emerging neighborhoods or properties with untapped potential, always looking to blaze new trails in the real estate market.

House Managers confidently lead the house hunt, but they lead with rational arguments rather than feelings. If homebuying were a start-up company, the House Manager would be its CEO. They delegate in all aspects of their lives. That extends to real estate agents, whom they hire as quickly as they can feel confident in their abilities. After that's done, and they select a neighborhood, they are no longer concerned with details. While they may appear aggressive in their appearance, House Managers are better able to bring together complicated real estate deals, because they are relentless. They always keep the outcome in mind and are the last to give up on a deal.

A first-time House Manager's overconfidence can look like selfish arrogance and can rub Homebodies and Good Neighbors the wrong way. If you are a House Manager, you must enroll everyone else in the powerful vision of your new home, or you will lose them in your brashness.

🏠 🏠 🏠

Jesse was an accountant by day, but a House Manager by night. He told me exactly what he wanted to buy: a three-bedroom apartment that needed a full renovation near the up-and-coming Hudson Yards neighborhood. He was ready to move, but given that he and his wife were renting, he was also willing to wait for the right opportunity. His wife, Nina, a Homebody, was willing to go along, since he had sold her on their move from Los Angeles to New York by promising her a home close to their daughter's school, done exactly to her specifications.

Within a few weeks, we found a combined high-floor loft that was being returned to its component parts—one being a lovely three-bedroom—and had just been discounted. In its dilapidated state, no other buyers were able to conceptualize what each part would look like after they were separated. Except I had a secret weapon. My close friends lived in a finished version of the exact same apartment a few floors below. That helped seal the deal. In concept, anyway.

But then the sale of their home in Los Angeles was delayed due to a construction defect. Jesse wasn't apologetic or flustered, though. He was calm, matter-of-fact, and, to my frustration, went radio silent on me for about two weeks before I ran down what was going on—right in the middle of a contract negotiation. Then he went underground for three months, leaving me in limbo and the listing agent and his sellers looking for a new buyer.

Jesse worked out the kinks of his sell-side contract, and to his delight, no one had bought the loft during the intervening months. The trouble lay not in negotiating a lower sales price, but in convincing the sellers that my buyers were serious. They had been so abrupt in stepping back from the deal that I had a lot of apologizing to do. House Managers like Jesse get deals done, but they also have a tendency to burn bridges in their haste.

Here Goes the Neighborhood

How do you feel when you associate yourself with one buyer profile or another? Often, my clients will laugh at themselves when they recognize their own behavior in these descriptions. Less amusing is when they identify their spouse's or partner's profile because they are intimidated by how to best manage their relationship in a new setting, especially when money comes into play.

Opposites do attract, so don't get too frustrated that you and your partner's Buyer Personality Profiles are in conflict. While managing different personalities is an agent's cross to bear, managing your own interpersonal drama will likely be an ongoing challenge. We'll look at more complicated couple scenarios in chapter 5 where relationships are, shall we say, less evolved.

Hiring Your Advisor

Homebuying is inherently complicated, just as unforeseen snags and unforced errors are part of the process. I can't help but channel my inner Jay-Z in saying that, for all of the problems, you just don't want your agent to be one. As luck would have it, choosing an agent is a decision you can control.

How would it feel if every aspect of the homebuying process were tailored to your personality and communication style? Not just what properties you received, but how you received the information about them, delivered exactly when and how often you wanted. A partnership that inspires you and keeps you inspired about what is possible. A perfect balance between efficiency and relationship building. Communication that opens you up and builds trust. An ongoing conversation to also help you help yourself.

So take charge of your search. Armed with your Buyer Personality Profile, you already have an in-depth understanding of what you need in a partnership with a buyer agent. The last step is to officially hire one who speaks your language. How will you go about it? A reminder: Do not be part of the 71% of buyers who hire the first agent they meet. Be deliberate with your decision.

In the abstract, having an agent with the same perspective as you might seem very helpful. The alternative could be a House Manager getting very annoyed with a Good Neighbor agent who dedicates every conversation to relationship building. A Meter Reader might want to throw an impatient Designer agent out the window. What you want is an agent who keeps their natural instincts under control. Don't forget that agents are usually managing multiple Buyer Personalities. The best agents know how to manage them all at once.

It's up to you to determine how skillful they are in doing so. This decision-making starts before you even meet an agent. If you've been referred to them, how are they described? One buyer I interviewed told me, "I even got mixed messages from the people that worked with him." Needless to say, he didn't hire that person. Pay attention to how they respond to your outreach too. Does it feel like they're working for you, or working against you?

Here are a few questions to be thinking about as you evaluate each prospective agent:

1. *What kind of questions are they asking? Are they just the basics of the transaction, or are they trying to get to know you?*

    You already have a good framework for all the information that will be helpful to your search. Don't be afraid to redirect the discussion or share more details than were asked. See how the agent reacts.

2. *Do you feel comfortable around them? Do they answer your questions in a way that makes sense to you? Do you feel heard, seen, and understood? Take this a little further. Do you like the way that they speak to your partner or spouse?*

    Don't think before you answer. I suspect you'll just know in your bones whether this is or isn't a good fit. You'll soon confirm how your partner or spouse feels about them.

Whatever their reaction, it will be a helpful discussion to have. Remember, you're about to spend weeks, if not months (or longer!), in dialogue with them.

3. *Are you holding back in any area of the agent's questions? For instance, is the money part of the discussion strange in any way?*

A recent Zillow study reported that more than 50% of all buyers look to their agents to help them make financing decisions. Compare this to less than a third who look to banks or friends for financial advice. More often than not, buyers come to trust their agent more than they expect.

So, as awkward as it might be for your family dynamics, I would not recommend you hire your cousin to be your agent if you don't want to disclose your financial information. Alternatively, what if you find it exhausting to trust the highly recommended agent in front of you? Think about hiring a close friend to represent you instead.

4. *Who is leading the conversation? You or the agent?*

I know the essence of customer service is that the customer is always right, but I don't think this always needs to be true. I'll put this a different way. This agent is either an order taker or an advisor. If they are an order taker, they might only be willing to tell you what you want to hear. An advisor will step up and say what you *need* to hear. An advisor will also ask clarifying questions when they don't know enough to render an opinion. Which do you think this person is?

It's a balance. Your opinions and priorities matter far more than your agent's taste. Reflect on whether they seem to be in service to you or to themselves.

5. *Do you feel this agent is experienced enough?*

This part of the conversation can go in many ways. You may want to learn what type of sales listings the agent generally works with because it could be helpful if they are familiar with the kinds of homes you're looking for, and the personalities of those looking for those homes. It can also help them determine if your finances are in line with your expectations.

There's also a decent chance that you'll meet a new agent, since 20% of all agents working today are in their first two years in the business. That's not a disqualification, though. Just know that new agents don't tend to work with buyers because it is easier. They only start there because buyer clients are so much *easier to find* than sellers. So make sure you ask enough questions to get comfortable around their work ethic. I think it's a good indication how quickly they are learning the skills to help you.

A good rule of thumb is, at the very least, to hire a full-time agent. Bear in mind that the average Realtor works only 30 hours per week, according to a poll of the National Association of Realtors' members, and real estate agents who defined *themselves* as part-time in a separate poll work less than *20* hours per week. These numbers worry me, because for new agents, so much of residential real estate is apprenticeship. There is almost no overlap between the information needed to pass a real estate licensing exam and the information needed to be a good real estate agent. Guy Gal, the CEO of real estate services firm Side, which powers over 600 independent real estate brokerage firms, did a little digging in his local market and discovered this: More than 70% of all residential sales in San Francisco in 2023 were done by agents who did only three deals that year. Does such extreme part-time practice qualify agents to effectively manage your purchase, let alone claim to have a finger on the pulse of the market? I assert that it does not.

6. *How do they follow up after your meeting?*

Is their follow-up slow or nonexistent? Did they thank you for meeting with them, or even proactively send a few ideas after your meeting? No matter how highly recommended an agent comes, or how many awards they've won, if you don't feel like you're important to them, you're sunk before you leave port.

🏠 🏠 🏠

With your conversations and post-meeting wrap-up discussions completed, make your commitment. You have influence, knowledge, and power over your choice of agent. This is momentous! You're already applying what you've learned about yourself. You are creating a team that is mission-oriented and purpose-driven. It's not complicated, nor should it be. This is a framework you can use in any price range and in any city. Take comfort in knowing you're doing all you can to ensure a better experience. Crafting relationships like those I've described will do more to improve your outcome than any lawsuit, adjustment to the Multiple Listing Service, implementation of buyer representation agreements, or other drastic overhauls of the buyer–seller business model.

Making this commitment may not be so cut-and-dried, however. If you're looking in towns not near enough to each other to encompass one person's expertise, you could end up hiring more than one agent. I give you permission to even test-drive two agents in the *same* location (which is a good sign that you're a Meter Reader, by the way). There is also a chance that you will hire the wrong agent. It happens. Breaking up with them is a tricky matter, but rip off that Band-Aid. A few minutes of uncomfortable discussion are better than sticking with someone who is the wrong fit. On behalf of agents everywhere,

I beg you not to do this by email or text. Clearing the air even a little is good practice for all of the other gnarly conversations you'll have going forward.

Don't limit yourself to where you apply this hiring wisdom either. Why not engage the same rigor when you hire your real estate attorney (where applicable), bring in your mortgage broker, and, if you're doing work to a house, source recommendations for contractors, architects, and designers? They each provide a slice of the supportive structure, information, advice, and feedback critical to your success going forward. Think also of your personal circle, the nonprofessionals whom you involve in your home search. How can you clarify what you need from them, and how and when they give it to you? We still have a way to go, and a team rowing in the same direction will go farther, faster.

Now we must return to the search itself, which, like the open house, is a liminal space. As much self-exploration as you might have done so far, are you sure you know what you want? And where do all these preferences come from, anyway?

CHAPTER 4

There Is No Free Will
in Real Estate

And How to Make Good Real

Estate Decisions Anyway

*"Welcome to my house! Enter freely
and of your own free will!"*
—Count Dracula

The House Rules

Checklist? Check. Agent? Hired. Readiness meter? Set on inspired. Property tour? Set. And continuing our riff on agents as coaches—and buyers as players—you're out of the locker room and on the court for tip-off, bursting with enthusiasm when you arrive at your first private appointment.

Here we go, you say to yourself as your agent takes the keys from the lockbox and opens the front door. *Gee, it's so quiet in here. Was I excited during that open house last week, or was I just feeling the boozy brunch we came from?* You look around. You move from room to room like a zombie. *Wait! Why does this feel like I'm hate-watching television right now?* And each house is worse than the last. After the appointments, you will try to explain to your agent why you didn't like the properties, even though they all, theoretically anyway, had everything on your list. You come up with some reasons. *I guess I hadn't expected that number one on today's list would need that much work. The backyard of the second wasn't as nice as I hoped. The garage of the third one felt a little small, didn't it?*

You know why you're moving. And you were sure what your new home should look like. Except you don't like what you thought you would like! Comedian John Mulaney described this mismatch, and the fundamental flaw of this stage of your home search, as follows:

> I like having a house, but I loved looking for a house, because I love real estate agents. I mean, they are the true heroes. They really are. Have you ever watched HGTV? Real estate agents have to deal with the dumbest people in the world making the biggest decisions of their lives.
>
> Every episode of HGTV is like, "Craig and Stacia are looking for a two-story A-frame that's near Craig's job in 'the downtown,' but also satisfies Stacia's need to be near the

beach, which is nowhere near Craig's job. With three children and nine on the way, and a max budget of seven dollars . . . let's see what Lori Jo can do on this week's episode of *You Don't Deserve a Beach House.*"

Does Mulaney really think you're dumb? Of course not. But he does a hilarious job of at least pointing out that something is off. I've also heard real estate professionals try to express what they think is going on, except their explanation is not funny at all: *Buyers are liars.* Pretty sinister, and also wrong. What these agents miss is that no one is lying to them. How can you be dishonest when you don't know what you want?

I'd ask you to review the Your Big Idea section of the chapter 2 Buyer Intake Questionnaire again. Have you ever stopped to consider when exactly you started liking one style of house over another, or why you prefer an open kitchen to a closed one? Even if you thought everything you have shared was the God's Honest Truth, how do you verify that?

You can't. In *Thinking, Fast and Slow,* cognitive scientist Daniel Kahneman claims (and his Nobel Prize–winning research proved) that your true preferences lurk behind a series of "non-rational motivations or triggers." These triggers will not usually steer you in the right direction. Another way to say this is that, despite all the work you've done to create your vision of a home so far, there is no free will in real estate. If you want to learn what will make you happy, you will need to fathom how little agency you have in the matter. Then we will forge a far easier path to your dream house.

The Roots of Your Real Estate Preferences

Jackie and her husband, Sandy, toured no fewer than 50 apartments, covering every option along Central Park West below 96th Street.

This 30-block stretch features some of the toniest, most elegant buildings Manhattan has to offer. The home they finally chose peered out
over the Jacqueline Kennedy Onassis Reservoir from their living
room, situated within a luxury art deco landmark designed by Emery
Roth, a famous architect of the late 1920s. Its highlights: striking
lobby murals, gold-leafed ceilings, and even authentic period furniture. Were this not enough of what passes for curb appeal in New
York City, each elevator landing, shared by at most two apartments,
featured a carefully crafted mosaic floor.

These lifetime New Yorkers could admire the building's history
and its details. What others casually discarded in renovations, they
celebrated, elements such as the original "bullet hinge" brass door
hardware and sturdy metal St. Charles cabinets that have been wildly
popular since the company's 1935 founding. Jackie and Sandy liked
the past. It was a reference point from which they could better appreciate how far they had come.

One Sunday morning, they traveled along Ocean Parkway toward
Jackie's childhood haunts in Midwood, the middle-class neighborhood in south-central Brooklyn where she was raised and which they
regularly visited. Jackie would normally just point out the building
where she grew up to her children. But this time, she asked Sandy
to pull over. She joked with her kids, "Why don't we just ring the
bell and see if anyone is in our old apartment?" She didn't expect the
woman living there to buzz her in.

They walked through the lobby and piled into the elevator, giddy
in anticipation. As the elevator door slid open, though, she stared
down at the tile floor, gobsmacked. The mosaic was *identical* to that
of her current apartment landing. The same pattern, the same colors,
everything. She had subconsciously re-created her happy Brooklyn
upbringing in her new home.

Like Jackie, you have a yet-untapped world of memories and emotions influencing your real estate desires. Forget the old checklist and the first draft of your vision. Put motivation aside. What will make you feel like you've come home? How do you go about answering this question, when you don't even know what you know or remember? A mosaic tile floor could bring out the happy thoughts of a six-year-old version of yourself who, apparently, is pulling the strings in your home search! Alternatively, you may have an adverse reaction to a kitchen solely because it reminds you of an off-putting detail of your childhood hidden somewhere in your memories.

There are more than a few hidden preferences that can keep you from a successful outcome. You'll need to work to get past what you cannot control—which is just about everything—to detect those details that make a house feel like a home.

From the Cave to the Cottage

To do so, we must go under the hood. Much of your conception of home was hardwired into your brain long before you were born, and long before humans were even *Homo sapiens*. I'll try to spare you the in-depth science class, but here are the basics: Our primitive ancestors could not count on food, shelter, or safety. Banding together didn't guarantee these needs, either, but it increased the odds. Out of those groups came a sense of belonging and a desire to both care for and be cared for by its members. As we evolved, the hearths of those caves became stages for storytelling, their walls easels for memory, their nooks storehouses for tools.

If you think about it, our homes today are only nicer versions of that same cave. Our relationship to our tribe hasn't changed much either. Not only do we still need to stay connected to it, but we must know where we fit into its pecking order. Status-seeking through the homes we own is commonly known in America as "keeping up with the Joneses." This sets into motion an arms race that includes our front lawns, or the hedges that obscure them, or the makes and models parked in our driveways. Our houses are among the most prominent status symbols we have, from the prestige of certain neighborhoods, to the country club–like application process of cooperative buildings in New York City.

Despite my best efforts, I just gave you many of the components of well-known psychologist Abraham Maslow's *hierarchy of needs* anyway. But rather than self-actualization as the peak of that pyramid, your dream house is the cherry on top. Ironically, the home search undermines all you've achieved: your safety, food security, feelings of belonging and connection to your tribe, and your sense of place in it. The hunt gets intense. Your well-meaning friends and family unwittingly add pressure. Then your lizard brain, or amygdala, goes on high alert, and you go into survival mode. That leaves you three options: fight, flight, or freeze. While brilliantly devised for avoiding the tiger attacks faced by our early ancestors, not one of those options helps with house hunting.

The Hackathon

You have also been primed to cede control of your decision-making, courtesy of marketers, television producers, social media content creators, and other master manipulators.

Even theme park operators know how to pull your levers in your home search. Venture no further than Main Street, U.S.A., Walt Disney World's curated opening scene. It is a re-creation of Disney's childhood home of Marceline, Missouri—with a few important changes. The old-timey storefronts, with their hand-painted signage, are a shade smaller than they would otherwise be in real life. Their scale gives the target audience—children—a sense of mastery of their environment, and, through that, feelings of comfort. Author Karal Ann Marling dubbed it the "architecture of reassurance." The Happiest Place on Earth has been toying with your emotions about home, all the way to the cash register.

I use this example because real estate design plays an enormous role in our feeling of calm, starting in childhood. As adults, we still strongly prefer comfort over the distracting, disconcerting, and unfamiliar. This plays out anytime a Board of Overseers, or whatever your town's elected commission happens to be called, tries to do its job. This reflex engages, too, when a private group of outraged citizens coalesces to say, "Not in my backyard." Both are attempting to enforce the architecture of reassurance. Municipalities are constantly devising or floating zoning laws that may ignore competing desires of affordability, diversity, and, at its most basic, your individual expression.

🏠 🏠 🏠

The 1950s in America welcomed network television into the home, and the golden age of marketing began. With it came the tradition known as product placement. As a result, you have been exposed to between 4,000 and 10,000 advertisements *per day*, every day of your life. The background for nearly every product promotion, sitcom, or movie is a kitchen, living room, or bedroom scene. By my math, that's some 30 million real estate images seared into your eyeballs before you're of legal drinking age. This is to say that Madison Avenue and Hollywood hacked your gray matter long before you ever thought about buying a home.

Like brand managers and copywriters, reality television producers also use market research to play your needs to their advantage.

For example, the producers of Home & Garden Television's home improvement programming in the late 1990s noticed their viewing audience was growing, but it was nearly all female. Then they happened upon what would get men to sit down next to them for the shows: demolition. On the 25th anniversary of HGTV, National Public Radio mainstay Lulu Garcia-Navarro and *New York Times* journalist Ronda Kaysen discussed the now-ubiquitous "open concept house" that we all know—and have been persuaded to love:

> The reason that they are so big on "open concept" is because it gets the male viewers . . . Kaysen added, "Guys like to watch sledgehammers and, like, taking out walls." HGTV decision-makers feel that straight men won't sit down with their girlfriends and wives for an hour of tchotchkes and bathroom upgrades if they can't catch a little sledgehammer action along the way. "It's for TV," Kaysen said. "It's not for, like, what's in the best interests of the house, necessarily."

It may not be what you want either. Tastes have changed, perhaps, but not the physics of sound. You don't have to be remotely elderly to notice the decibel level, and outright cacophony, of restaurants, classrooms, and other open spaces you frequent in public life. Just try to enjoy a dialogue-driven drama without subtitles on any streaming service while your partner is frying an egg in what is effectively the same room. At least half of my clients tell me they prefer to keep their dirty dishes out of sight in a *closed* kitchen! Do you? Yet those sledgehammers continue to swing.

Let's step back to examine just how pervasive reality television is. It represents 73% of all programming across cable and broadcast networks. To be fair, the top reality shows are not directly related to real estate. But they all include a real estate component. Real Housewives must all live somewhere, just as Top Chefs must cook in their kitchens. America's most talented all have a backstory that takes you into their childhood homes. And the cameras follow the romantic escapades of bachelors or bachelorettes as they cohabitate, even if their relationships don't last much longer than their episodes.

Real estate reality television itself has vast penetration into the American mind. Its top-rated shows get close to a million viewers *per minute*. Eleven million people visit HGTV's website monthly, and nearly 44 million view its programming per month, nearly all of which is real estate or real estate–adjacent reality TV. Its ratings have never been higher. To call this brainwashing might be uncharitable, but after two decades, design ideas such as open-concept layouts are, for better or worse, burned into our retinas.

Since the producers of these potentially counterfeit visions of living prioritize near-term Nielsen ratings far more than any long-term hopes of your satisfaction, there is a cost to playing along. What the buyers on the screen want becomes social proof of what *everyone* wants—and what you should want too. Dr. Maxwell Maltz, in his groundbreaking book *Psycho-Cybernetics*, sees it like this: "[E]very human being is hypnotized to some extent either by ideas he has uncritically accepted from others or ideas he has repeated to himself or convinced himself are true."

We have come to the belief that buying and selling homes is a 30-minute affair, made worse by the foolish notion that every home mimics this experience. All aspects of renovation are glossed over or misrepresented in one way or another, from the need for it (hidden by staging), to the cost of it, to the speed in which it can be completed. No decently constructed kitchen, bath, or bedroom takes an afternoon to build. Most contractors would tell you that a budget of $20,000 will not get you an entire home makeover, even in a studio apartment or in the least expensive housing market in the United States. Reality can be a big disappointment.

There is, however, a potential upside to reality: You will get more than three properties to choose from, and as long as you need to visit them. The variety of home furnishings is also far broader than what is on television. But having more options isn't always better, as the folks at Costco know all too well.

🏠 🏠 🏠

Social media has done some hypnotizing of its own, though before I sling more mud, I want to share one of its positive contributions: the recent shift replacing the word *master* in "master bedroom" or "master bath" with the more neutral word *primary* in 2020. There were no state laws in place to enforce a change from one to the other. They proved unnecessary because memes disseminated this real estate knowledge like wildfire. Instead, these phrases representing what some felt were subtle or not-so-subtle shades of racism or sexism were erased almost overnight. Pre–social media, this shift in attitude and subsequent adoption might have taken years.

But like reality television, social media has homogenized and limited the styles of home interiors that you'll see and that will feed, or starve, your creativity. The more you react to certain images and home tour videos, the more the algorithms curate similar images and videos. Some will go viral, and the whittling process continues across billions of posts. The tyranny of the *like* button drastically limits the variety of real estate in the world, and on your screen. This sameness extends to home furnishings. The jury's out whether your smartphone is in fact listening to your kitchen table conversations. Just as with fashion, however, interior design hasn't only trickled into big-box retail, but overwhelmed your social media feed, complete with baked-in shopping links.

Social media has also further democratized the age-old jealousy so cautioned against in the Ten Commandments. Just as you didn't know what you were missing socially before every detail of your friends' lives were publicly online, now, more than ever, you're constantly exposed to how the one percent of the one percent lives. All you have to do is open Instagram. *Lifestyles of the Rich and Famous*, a massively popular once-a-week program in the 1980s, looks so quaint compared to the intimate view of wealth we have today. The homes we can afford may appear shabby by comparison.

Opposite Mode

Somewhere along the line, you started playing someone else's game of house. You won't have to view many homes before this battle between your brain and your heart becomes evident, and for your heart to try to take back control. I would describe this as a contradiction that doesn't quite compute. Out of your unmet expectations comes an eddy of confusion, frustration, and anxiety. Psychologists call it cognitive dissonance. As the smoke comes out of your ears, the typical response will be to point out everything that you deem wrong in a house. I call it Opposite Mode. It comes in direct conflict with attraction-based buying, though both are essential components of The Magnetic Method.

Noticing what is absent or defective in every home you visit provides its own alluring certainty as a replacement for your disappointment. You are building a case, a justification rooted in your growing doubt for why this home *just doesn't work*. It starts with a tiny crack in a wall, a dated wedding photo over the sofa, a college diploma hanging in the home office, or a too-revealing pregnancy photo that someone turned into bedroom art. It could be as innocent as one misplaced piece of mail, address up, that can transport you from *I can see myself here* to *Oh, I know these people.* (If this also sounds like What Not To Do staging advice for sellers, it is.)

I have seen so many clients get turned off from properties I had been certain they would like. Since I represent sellers, too, I am constantly soliciting feedback from buyers or their agents after viewings. These agents are often equally baffled that the property missed the mark. My perspective, after two decades of selling real estate, is that whatever the stated reasons, they are usually *excuses*.

The actual reasons are often completely random and entirely irrational. Sometimes it's the weather. An off-putting smell in the lobby. A listing agent who showed up late, seemed irritated to be there, or talked too much during our tour. Other times I could see that my client's work email blew up during a viewing and they completely forgot they were even looking at houses. Or even something less visible—perhaps it was something they ate. Studies have demonstrated that courtroom judges, trained to be rational, are still more lenient in their sentencing after breakfast, and again after lunch. Why would buyers be any better? However they slipped into Opposite Mode, the opportunity to fall in love with that particular home is lost forever.

None of it has anything to do with what you have stated that you liked in your visioning exercise. You are rationalizing an emotional reaction to a home with whatever excuse jumps out of your brain. It has nothing to do with free will, nor anything to do with how many boxes a house checks off or how motivating your agent is. Face it. You don't really know what your dream house looks like yet, any more than you know who the "perfect" person will be when you're on the dating scene. And like dating, you can't really articulate why you swipe left or right. It's chemical. It's chemistry. It happens way too fast. You will invent the disqualifications later—anything to stop your friend's post-date interrogation. Sure, they were all *too something* and *not enough something else.* You will see the light when the person you fall in love with was all the things you told yourself you didn't want. It's the same in your house hunt. You might be startled at what entrances you—or repels you.

♦ ♦ ♦

Take my clients Mel and Sherry, classic Meter Readers if you're still keeping tabs on Buyer Personalities, who spent nearly a year in Opposite Mode. From Sherry I would hear about the too-low ceiling heights, incorrect orientation of windows, awkward layout, lack of closet space, or wrong type of flooring. Mel was driven more by spreadsheets than bedsheets. If the listing agent didn't have on-the-spot answers to his detailed fact-finding questions, he knocked that apartment off the list. He only trusted Realtors who had *answers*. He expected homebuying to be an equation with an exact result at the end and was hugely disappointed when the answers were not tidy. In the world of analytics, the phrase goes, "garbage in, garbage out." In the world of your home search, you also get out what you put in. If you only compile and input information about what you *dislike*, your algorithm will only give you a negative number. There's no room to learn what you would love.

Mel and Sherry's combined dislikes—and excuses—canceled out nearly every viable option. Lots of homes came very, very close, but not close enough. Neither could ignore the minutiae. They languished in Opposite Mode for nearly a year as they tried to re-create the apartment they had lived in for 20 years and just sold, when what they wanted was to walk in and feel a new emotional connection. They found that spark in a lovely high-floor apartment, which happened to be in a building where her sister already lived.

♦ ♦ ♦

To add to your confusion, you may still be deliberating about where you want to live. The statistics say you are more likely to land in the suburbs. But this decision is never just about the house you choose. Moving to a new town, or even a new neighborhood, adds a layer of complexity to your version of Opposite Mode. It's not always obvious what might be bothering you.

Environmental psychologist Ann Sloan Devlin, in her 2010 book *What Americans Build and Why*, offers a slew of reasons why you're bothered before you even walk into a house. I have no bone to pick with The Walt Disney Company, but Devlin again offers one of their biggest experiments—the town of Celebration, Florida—as an example. Despite including the best ideas of urban design, many of its residents interviewed still felt that it was somehow *too new*. Think of movies like *The Truman Show*, *Edward Scissorhands*, or *Don't Worry Darling*. A thousand houses built all at once, along with their shiny driveways, identical mailboxes, and matching roof shingles, will lack the patina of a neighborhood that evolved over years and years. Even too few mature trees can disturb your peace of mind. Buyers express this sentiment in new condo buildings, too, when they say, "This feels like a hotel," and mean it as a bad thing. More commonly, someone tells me a property feels too "cookie cutter."

Perhaps where you're looking does not have a true town center, or even a clear sense of its outer limits. What if there are no sidewalks? Would that impart an unspoken feeling of isolation? If you've ever wondered what "walkability scores" are on real estate websites, this is what they're talking about. A home without a porch may itself induce a negative reaction. How will you meet your neighbors? It's not something you might immediately discern, but without a porch, you intuit that the home lacks the layout for natural interactions.

Feeling lost in a neighborhood or even in a house could indicate a poor job of what is known as wayfinding. That could scare you off.

On the other hand, psychologists Stephen and Rachel Kaplan posit that a lack of nature might be creating mental fatigue. So if you feel exhausted looking at a house, maybe you need more than a backyard. You need more isolation, farther away from the city.

Related to safety, there have been studies that show that too-tall neighborhood hedges can spark fears of someone lurking right behind them. I suffer from an adjacent fear. There is something about the big windows on the ground floor of a single-family home that makes me feel exposed and uncomfortable. My wife and I both grew up in houses in the suburbs, but she cannot understand this irrational alarm. Nor can I! No doubt, had we chosen to look for a house to live in rather than an apartment, my reactions would have frustrated us both to no end.

Articulating exactly why a home feels too small may not be easy, since it can be like the famous quote by Supreme Court Justice Potter Stewart on obscenity: You only know it when you see it. It might not be the overall size, either, but *where* properties are shrinking. In some cases, the separate dining room is going extinct. In other construction, the open kitchen has, in effect, eaten the living room. Elsewhere, living rooms have narrowed as televisions have gotten thinner. In fact, newly built one-bedroom apartments have lost over 100 square feet on average, a reduction of more than 10% since 2000. So it's not just your imagination.

Alternatively, what if a home is just too large? A lack of coziness could be the culprit. For as much as people claim to love the "great room," and for all the popularity of McMansions, the tiny den is, for many, still the most important room in their house. Culturally speaking, Europeans like their bedrooms smaller, while Americans like their boudoirs the size of studio apartments. It turns out that how you perceive the size and space of a room is impacted by your country of origin. So the home you just scratched off your list could just be a mismatch based on your background, and nothing more.

As irritating and whimsical as you might seem to real estate agents while in Opposite Mode, you're even more annoying to your partner. It's worth drilling down on the teamwork element of the home search, given that upward of 70% of homebuyers are a couple of some kind. These dynamics play an outsized role in keeping you in Opposite Mode.

Plenty of couples already butt heads about where they want to live. And practical considerations such as a change of employment, affordability, pregnancy, or the quality of school systems may not hit you with the same level of immediacy as they do your partner. It can be unsettling, and confusing, when your sense of urgency doesn't match theirs. I recently discussed this with a couple who were selling their apartment in the city and buying a home in Connecticut. The husband had been ready to move for years. Despite having two young children, the wife was, however, in his words, "still living in a fantasy where she was in her twenties and going out every night with her friends." Until she accepted that their lives had already shifted into a calmer gear, she couldn't get on that train to the suburbs, in a manner of speaking.

As it happens, Opposite Mode serves both helpful and unhelpful purposes. It is yet another way to hold on to what has been, and who you were before you started your hero's journey. Eckhart Tolle puts it beautifully when he writes, "The habitual and reactive 'no' strengthens the ego. 'Yes' weakens it."

But here's the kicker: Whining and complaining about properties—and each other—is only the outward representation of Opposite Mode. Under the surface, each of you is sifting through all this information. You are pumping the brakes until your left brain catches up to your right brain, until your reason catches up with your feelings and intuitions. So, before you get any angrier at each other, give yourself the gift of patience to process what you are learning. Because you have been slowly aligning your property magnet all along.

The Power of the Offer

To cheer up that impatient part of you, and perhaps to diminish its hold over you, we need to turn one more piece of accepted wisdom on its head. Specifically, *follow your bliss*, which was also coined, for better or worse, by the same Joseph Campbell behind the hero's journey. The conventional assumption is that there is a career, a partner, or a house out there that will bring you profound delight, if you would only find and follow some bright yellow brick road to get there. However, even Campbell knew his catchy catchphrase was misunderstood. In truth, it works, but only as a *retrospective* process. The randomness of life must take you through a variety of jobs, dates, breakups, and experiences that you won't like. Only later will you incorporate what you love, a process that often takes decades.

We don't have decades for your search, and, luckily, we don't need them. In homebuying, you have one critical advantage over a career search or quest for a loved one. You've gotten past the prequel portion of the house hunt, as it were, because you have been training for this journey since birth. Think about your childhood homes and those of your friends: ranch houses, Cape Cods, townhomes, Colonials, Craftsmans, farmhouses, Greek revivals, Tudors, Victorians, and apartment buildings. The vacations and summers that took you to camp cabins, ships' cabins, and RVs. When you left the nest, you lived in dorm rooms, rented your first apartment, and on you went from there. Your life has been a series of real estate classrooms and test-drives, during which you have already developed many or all of your unconscious preferences.

And really, there are no groundbreaking decisions to be made in real estate. How dissimilar are the ruins of ancient houses from the layouts we build today? Only improvements in technology, materials, and construction techniques separate us. Truly, your every preference is based on some precondition or reaction. Yet we have the persistent belief that we need to reinvent the wheel in our home search, when all we need is to develop the ability, in the words of Maslow, to be "independent of the good opinion of others." You have the option to trust yourself, no matter what your heart is telling you, no matter how people react to your choices. In real estate, you do get to follow your bliss.

My mind drifts to one of the most pioneering people I ever met—my diminutive grandmother. Grandma Millie, as I called her, would regale me with stories that revealed her willingness to go against the grain in life, and in her real estate. My grandfather Henry was a traveling salesman who was away for weeks at a time. During one of his business trips, Millie found, and bought, a bigger house in her South Florida neighborhood to fit their family of five, which by then included my mother. This passed for salacious stuff in the 1950s, far too juicy for her coffee klatch to ignore. Her girlfriends were confident that he was going to divorce her. She laughed it off.

Years later, she dipped her toe into real estate development on the Florida Intracoastal by building a new house for her family. Had you been in Millie's social group, you would have recognized the house she built. Because she tracked down the architect who had designed a house she liked—her friend Shirley's house—and had him create a copy. I wondered aloud whether that ruffled her friends' feathers. Ever the House Manager (in the parlance of Buyer Personalities), she shrugged and said, "Shirley shouldn't have been so mad. She should have been flattered."

That long-ago real estate deal, and the subsequent construction project, eventually sold for a hundred times what it cost her. But the money is not the point, nor is being original. What mattered was that she was a shrewd, strong, practical woman who, knowing her own mind, acted confidently and didn't seem to care what anyone else thought about it. John Stuart Mill once wrote, "That so few now dare to be eccentric, marks the chief danger of the time." That is still true today. Embrace your eccentricity, your unique likes and dislikes. They will lead you to a house you love. The hazards of the 1950s housewife seem so innocent when peer pressure today comes through social media like a fire hose. With one swipe, you can compare yourself to your neighbors and friends, and come to believe that you're the only one who hasn't cracked the code. How do you develop an independent streak, then? How will you take bold action? It all boils down to letting go of what you think you want. I will share a solution to bypass your frustrations and your misplaced expectations. It will skirt around both your internal software's programming and those who would use it for their own benefit. It will even short-circuit Opposite Mode. And you will quickly learn what desires and wishes have thus far escaped you. The antidote to this tailspin of negativity is making offers.

Think of offers not as a commitment, but as a real-life psychology experiment happening in real time. At every step, you will gain clarity about your needs. In New York City, neither party is committed to a purchase until contracts have been signed by both buyer and seller. If you live anywhere else, you might be screaming at the page, "Wait, what? I can't just make offers willy-nilly!" That's because, in some housing markets, offers are legally binding.

But not exactly. In markets with strict offer protocols (check with your agent about yours), you can still have in-depth—though informal as need be—conversations with listing agents that comfortably substitute for what I'm proposing. As you and your agent discuss a seller's informal reaction to your inquiry, you'll get to see how you feel about it too. There is nothing to reason out. Whatever appears is your answer. More than that, though, a savvy suburban buyer I interviewed called his accepted offer a "thousand-dollar option to buy the house." What he meant was that while the offers were deemed contracts where he lived, the inspection still gave him an out. He and his wife would use the post-inspection negotiation to walk away if they changed their mind. Even better, binding offers serve another purpose. Assuming you remain head over heels with the house, you're protected from competition. Buyers don't get that protection in New York City without fully executed contracts.

What Your Offers Should Include:

- The basics—price and terms
- Your logic to back up your offer
- Your mortgage preapproval
- A little about your financials, so the seller believes you can close the deal
- *Optional: A little about you

I must briefly pull this bus to the side of the highway, because one question is likely nagging at you: How do you make an offer? Let's not get into the particular customs of any one market. Just know this: The offers you put forward should contain more than a number and deal points, though that is certainly step 1. Step 2 is to back your offer up with some logic, so that the listing agent—and then the seller—can evaluate your position. That is, why is your offer at that level? Lastly, and I might get in hot water for saying this, your offer should contain a little about you—anything that will help a seller envision you as their buyer. What do I mean? Not how much you love the home, though you can write some kind of love letter separately. No. Give them reasons to believe that you will be able to cross the finish line. State your joint income if you think it will help. Tell them you are preapproved and include the lender letter that shows it. Tell them you are flexible to their need to delay or speed up a closing. Work closely with your agent to determine how to approach this seller and their agent. That may require a phone call or two, but your offer will stand out. Sellers need not have a vision of home, but a vision of a qualified buyer. Make yourself that buyer. And let The Magnetic Method bring you together.

Instead of fighting against Opposite Mode, use it to your advantage. I created a worksheet called the Offer Feedback Tool, available online (at pursueyourhome.com/offerfeedbacktool) and in the appendix of this book. Section 1 leverages all of your feedback while in Opposite Mode. It has two columns, one titled "What I Don't Like," the other "What I Would Love." Go ahead and document everything negative that you find about the houses you visit, and what kinds of finishes, fixtures, and flooring you would never want to see in your next home. That should be a breeze. Now pour your energy into translating column 1 into the things you would absolutely love.

Organize your answers. Have your priorities shifted? Go and look at the original questionnaire you completed from chapter 2 and use this as a jumping-off point for your "What I Would Love" list. Write whatever comes to mind, even if some of the original things remain. Then circle the 10 things you wrote down that excite you the most.

Think of this not as gospel, but, at worst, a better-informed guideline than your original checklist. Your goal is to lay bare what is still hidden from view, and to fold it into a second draft of your vision. Diving back into your home search parameters, limit yourself to a small geographic area to start. That way, you can become educated about the practical items along the way: what value looks like in that neighborhood or town, what kinds of houses are on the market, and what they tend to sell for. A tighter radius helps you avoid being overwhelmed by too much information. Along the way, as soon as a house checks six of the ten boxes on your new Top 10 List—my recommended minimum threshold—make an offer on it. No house will be perfect. And, unless it's at the asking price, opening offers are rarely accepted, anyway.

The most important thing is that you listen to your inner wisdom at each step of the offer process. Marie Kondo's runaway bestseller *The Life-Changing Magic of Tidying Up* would call this noticing the things that "spark joy." A seller's response could make you angry or excited. You may be sincerely deflated by their lack of flexibility. You might be maximally nervous about losing the house, or you might not feel anything at all. What are sellers communicating? What is their agent saying? Does anyone seem anxious, confident, or overly cocky? Is the mood of the market trending in one direction or the other? Is every seller responding to your offers in exactly the same way? Maybe you are consistently bidding too low. All of this is handy, even crucial information to guide your future offers.

Agents educate themselves in very much the same way, except only you have access to the machinery of your mind. At worst, you will have air-kissed a few frogs. At best, you may even get your offer accepted. Either way, you win. You will be that much closer to finding your perfect home. Offers and counteroffers become the litmus test of whether or not you really love a house. Children's author Antoine de Saint-Exupéry wrote in *The Little Prince* that "it is only with the heart that one can see rightly: what is essential is invisible to the eye."

You may need to lose out on a deal before you find your footing, though. For example, a surgeon client was accustomed to operating under pressure, but this lifesaving calm did not serve his real estate goals. I warned him that we were competing with another buyer for a gorgeous Harlem townhouse we had bid on. I stressed that he needed to act quickly to sign a contract. He hesitated instead and was caught flatfooted when we were outbid. But he also learned what he liked about that house. We didn't miss out on the next one. Depending on the market you find yourself in, you may have to make lots of offers just to be competitive. You'll learn plenty, whether you enjoy it or not.

If you do exhaust what's on the market, or feel you've mastered what there is to learn about the original submarket, then expand your search. The only warning: The more offers you make, the more rejection you'll encounter. You might experience really bad behavior, which I'll touch on later. When you get that phone call from your agent, telling you that there are multiple bids over the asking price, or worse, that the seller is accepting someone else's, notice how you react. Take time to distinguish between wanting something because you can't have it and the pangs of genuine heartbreak.

Not even real estate agents can always tell the difference. My wife and I nearly lost out on the property we expected to be our first home together, even though our offer had already been accepted. The day we expected to sign the contract, the seller's agent called to tell me we had been outbid. Unless we increased our offer, they would be selling the property to someone else. I was devastated, as was my wife. The pit in my stomach was telling me one thing, as clear as day—to match their offer. We never regretted our choice.

It goes without saying that since you can't opt out of negotiations in real estate, you should attach yourself to an agent accustomed to bidding wars. The calm demeanor of a skilled negotiator can lessen the life-or-death quality these back-and-forth volleys often take on. Even more, can you treat them as a lighthearted game? The outcome is so often out of your control, so try to wear this attitude into battle rather than draping yourself in heavy armor. I leave it to you, your agents, and most importantly, your intuition to determine whether to take a lap, sleep on it, raise your bid, or walk away.

Last-minute jitters are normal (for sellers, too, by the way), but turn those nerves into a learning tool. Let your curiosity serve as a breakwater to the potentially overwhelming feelings that get in the way of thinking independently. And to reiterate, don't be afraid to back out of a deal. If this property isn't the one, you'll be even more ready next time.

Take detailed notes of everything you unearth. Give yourself the gift of integrating the learnings from each offer you make. I promise that they will be the basis of productive conversations with your real estate agent, your loved ones, and others. And if you're feeling particularly brave, take a rest from social media while you're at it. A digital fast doesn't have to be a sacrifice. It could be a wonderful indulgence. Leaving other people's opinions behind, even briefly, may be just the thing you need to hear what your heart has to say.

Learning by Ear

You've been banging the drum with that tired checklist for so long, wearing yourselves and your agent down in the process. Then something shifts as you make offers. Escaping Opposite Mode isn't a gradual catching-up either. It's instantaneous. One minute you were confused by your own reactions, and then you just "know" what works. That house you hated—if it's still on the market—is suddenly the perfect house. You start imagining new possibilities, where before you only saw what couldn't be. I cannot pinpoint when it will happen for you. But I can tell you why it happens: You're finally ready for what's next. It is the ultimate result of having Aligned your magnet. On some unspoken level, you have accepted that it is time to move. That acceptance gives you access to a different set of eyes and ears.

I'll show you what I mean by way of a group of bandmates trying to find their sound. Before real estate, I toured across the country as a singer in a professional a cappella group. We called ourselves a vocal band, but if you've ever seen the 2012 movie *Pitch Perfect* (produced by my college classmate, actress Elizabeth Banks, and her husband, Max Handelman, among others), we looked a lot more like the Barden Treblemakers than the Rolling Stones. One of many things the movie gets right about college a cappella groups, including their terrible names, is that they mostly perform popular music, not their own. That was true of the all-male ensemble I sang in during college, too, and no less so of professional all-vocal groups, which I learned as soon as I was auditioning to join one after graduation. The bulk of their repertoires were still cover songs. The difference, and what drew me to Ball in the House, other than my close friend Jason being in it, was that they wrote original music.

I won't bore you with the diva drama of six guys who all thought of themselves as lead singers. But we also had no drums, keyboards, guitars, or horns. This presented a production problem, when all we wanted was to emulate what most bands took for granted: a full sound. There we were, striving not only to be Lennon and McCartney, but to turn what were, in effect, four-part choral arrangements into radio-ready music. For a year, the best we could muster sounded hollow and weak, no matter who the front man was for a particular song.

Then, at an evening rehearsal, my bandmates Dave and Stephen came in with a ballad that our bass singer, Mike, had written and arranged. It had been seemingly pulled straight out of the Backstreet Boys' playbook: cheesy verse, heartstring-pulling lyrics, big, catchy chorus. Mike taught us the backing vocal *oohs* on piano, and our beatbox drummer, Jon, started to fill in with a 90-beat-per-minute slow-jam that was all over late '90s radio.

You could almost hear a *click* as everything came together. So badly had we wanted to overcome the sonic and structural limitations of the band, a task suddenly made irrelevant. We didn't intend to pen stripped-down R&B pop songs, nor hop on the boy band bandwagon. It was just the most authentic expression of our talents and what the songs needed in order to sound special.

Miles Davis is quoted as saying, "The hardest thing in music is to sound like yourself." We had come to this project with different emotional processing power, different priorities, and different musical tastes. It's hard enough for a couple to get in sync. It took a little longer for six singers to withdraw from Opposite Mode, to go from hating each other's arrangements to suggesting how to improve them. With that negative energy behind us, we, too, possessed a clearer vision, along with a new passion and drive to practice together more, tour more, and work even more energetically at our craft. More on my band's story later.

Try This at Home

Speaking of craftsmen, many judge Frank Lloyd Wright to be the father of the Arts and Crafts architectural movement and perhaps the greatest American architect of all time. I recently visited his Arizona desert studio, Taliesin West, which he completed in 1937. He left behind many original ideas, one of which was that architecture was the "great mother art" capable of transforming all of society. He was also of the opinion that only "true architecture" can nourish those who live within its walls. There I disagree. Homes don't have to be architecturally significant by anyone else's standards to have this power. They just have to be meaningful to you. And let's face it: Who builds all these houses, anyway? Not groundbreaking architects like Frank Lloyd Wright.

Well over a million homes are built each year in America. Entire neighborhoods and communities will rise from farmland, dead malls, and repurposed office parks. More than likely, your future home began its life as a *spec house*, built on the *spec*ulation that there will be a buyer ready to snap it up upon completion, or even before. At scale, most innovation is left on the cutting-room floor. One former C-suite employee of a publicly traded builder described the process to me as follows: "Study what is selling in an area, copy what works, give it a little nip and tuck—and lean on our reputation and the brand names (appliances, et cetera) to maximize the sale price of each home."

You could call this a flattening of design, a callous obsession with the bottom line, resulting in an ungodly crop of meta-houses influenced by social media, reality television, and technologies that alter how we live. Yet none of this is relevant. Spec homes have been and will always be the lifeblood of the homebuying journey. It never really mattered that every house on the street was once one of a handful of models, or that every floor of a building had the same six units stacked upon each other, anyway. From the art, furniture, and paint color, to the subsequent upgrades and expansions, they are immediately unique, and will only become more so.

You have no free will in what you think you want in your real estate, nor any in what you need. And that's okay. What makes your search fresh and exciting is when your past and your future collide in the present moment. It is in learning what inspires you, among all the preexisting ideas out there, that makes a home feel like it could be yours, like it will be yours. If you allow the search to proceed in this way, you will not reinvent the wheel, yet you will feel very much like Magellan—by becoming the explorer of your own heart. Then you only have to listen and watch. This clarity is the Attract component of The Magnetic Method in full effect.

Let this knowledge serve you and keep you pointed toward what you can control in your search, because your mind will soon create many other ingenious ways to complicate, and spice up, your real estate saga.

CHAPTER 5

Every House Becomes
a Guest House

How to Be a Good Host

*"The dark thought, the shame, the malice, meet
them at the door laughing, and invite them
in. Be grateful for whoever comes, because
each has been sent as a guide from beyond."*
—Rumi

The Fun House

Even the most efficient home search will be littered with dejection. Some offers you make will be laughed at or will fall on deaf ears. And at one point or another, yours will be the losing bid in a battle of interested parties.

What happens when a seller accepts your offer, though? Do you live happily ever after? Should you expect to feel the unbridled joy of Cubs fans celebrating their first World Series victory in a century? If you're a sci-fi fan, perhaps you're picturing the glee of hundreds of alien extras awkwardly dancing at the end of every Star Wars movie. I'm imagining the viral videos of the trick shot guys who jump up and down as if they just discovered fire.

Yet this theoretically glorious real estate achievement often prompts a distinctly nauseating reaction instead. You're like a greyhound at the racing track that actually caught the mechanical rabbit. Well, that wasn't supposed to happen! As the house dangles from your mouth, as it were, you don't know what to do next either. One single uncertainty—what kind of house am I going to find?—blossoms into a whole series of other thoughts. You're likely to feel even more out of control. I equate it to the overwhelm of being lost. I can still remember looking up for my mother's hand at four years old while at the zoo, only to suddenly register her absence. I was flooded with panic, a churning in my stomach, followed by the closing down of my field of vision, the flop sweat, and the nearly mute, no-eye-contact request to the security guard for help.

Your mind is furiously trying to unscramble the unknown future as the deal comes together. At this stage of the hero's journey, the hero, too, must decide what to do and whom to trust. And it's all coming too fast: information, negotiation, relocation, renovation, and decoration, not to mention the inspections, questions, and perhaps some indigestion. How do you handle a future you've never encountered before, when the only tools at your disposal are those that worked in the past? I'll tell you how: You'll try to fit these new experiences into old frameworks. The going gets tough, and your familiar feelings and thoughts get going, creating a variety of shutdowns, breakdowns, and meltdowns. Your outdated solutions are limiting beliefs that become obstacles of their own.

I am reminded of 13th-century poet Rumi's "The Guest House," in which he proposes that we think of our emotional reactions as guests who have come to visit us. These guests represent the familiar voices you have spent a lifetime internalizing: a judgmental sibling, a nasty aunt, an overbearing parent, a fearful friend, or, perhaps, your inner child. In their own way, they try to love you, protect you, and nurture you. Except their advice is catered perfectly to keep you looking backward—not oriented toward the task at hand. You need better tools. Better *emotional* tools to contend with them.

At every step, I have done my best to be encouraging and compassionate in sharing all that you are likely to face. So I must offer you a warning here: This is a rough part of the homebuying journey. Your guests are going to find ways to sabotage you and damage your property before you even own it. This is when the pressure of your emotions limits you, and gives you tunnel vision instead. Of course, I don't want the journey to seem so daunting that you're afraid to keep going. May I remind you that millions of people have gotten to the closing table with a fraction of the information you already have. Just know that while you'll resonate with some of these guests' behaviors, you'll learn from them too.

By the way, if you were hoping for a little more real estate kiss-and-tell, you'll thank me at the end of this chapter.

The Dealmaker

Any host will tell you that if a houseguest treats their home terribly, they are unlikely to get a second invitation. Therefore, there's no better place to start than with a poorly behaved houseguest, who also happens to be obsessed with a deal: the Dealmaker.

Everyone likes a bargain, but nowhere is this truer than in real estate. Come on, what greater joy could there be than to captivate a dinner party with the epic story of the home you believed you bought well under its market value? If the Dealmaker is your houseguest, he's been there all along. The telltale signs? You've been getting regularly outbid or, worse, getting silence from sellers when you submit offers.

The Dealmaker kicks into high gear after your offer is accepted. Linda is a perfect illustration. She started her search right before a recent market dip. Her lowball offers were laughed at—until they weren't. Soon, we had negotiated a price on an apartment 15% below what anyone had paid in the building in more than 10 years. When the contract was ready to be signed, however, she balked.

It was more than buyer's remorse. The Dealmaker had taken over. I could hear its voice in Linda's every question or comment. *Can't we do better than this? Are you sure we're not overpaying? The market may never recover from here, or it could get worse!* This self-talk may seem more trustworthy than that of your real estate agent, no matter how uninformed or unrealistic. For the Dealmaker speaks your language better than any agent could.

As you would expect, Linda did not go through with her transaction. Months later, she bought a lovely apartment, albeit without a discount. She had been so busy looking for a steal that she had missed the opportunity right under her nose. Be aware of your tendency to listen to the Dealmaker, especially if you have designated yourself as a Meter Reader. That combination will make you more naturally suspicious and mistrustful than most. And, more likely than not, you will end up where you started—paying a reasonable price for your home—and will have pointlessly put yourself through the wringer.

I've seen the Dealmaker's dirty work up close and personal. In 2007, my wife and I were newly married and expecting our first child, when I was offered a role as a salesperson on the team of a condominium tower project with a projected $350 million sellout. Still a newbie in the business, this promised to be a true home run for me. I had also agreed to buy a low-floor, two-bedroom unit in the project, even though I really didn't have the money to do so. I thought I could flip the contract just as I had seen my customers do, a practice that is far less common today. Better yet, the developers didn't require a good faith deposit of any kind when I signed the purchase agreement. They would let me apply the funds from my soon-to-be-earned commissions for the down payment.

Then this good situation transformed into a gift horse: The developers offered me $100,000 to assign my contract to one of their investors. That was when I should have said yes and walked away with *more money than I had ever made on any single deal before.* Instead, I got greedy and turned them down. Good fortune had fallen into my lap and, just as quickly, vaporized. Things only went from bad to worse. Within a few days, they fired me from the project, and as all good faith had already evaporated, they demanded earnest money for the contract to boot. It didn't take much longer for Lehman Brothers to collapse, the economy to fall apart, and for my fantasies of flipping the contract for a big profit to disappear. In its place was a fight to get out of the contract I had signed, in order to limit my losses. This humbling experience showed me how unskillfully the Dealmaker handles your blessings when put in charge.

The Pauper

Whatever your price point, and wherever you want to live, you will have to save for a down payment. And no matter the discipline of your money mindset, real estate dealings will instigate some flashpoints around the mighty dollar. The Dealmaker is the cocky cousin to the most common houseguest to appear at your doorstep: the Pauper. He is afraid that you don't, or won't, have adequate funds to afford your new home. I get his reaction too. You could be stretching yourself more than with any other investment you've ever made.

Tracy and Carter moved back to New York from the West Coast and into a one-year lease while they looked to buy. Two properties fit the bill, each squarely within their budget. Yet as the negotiations headed to what looked like a successful conclusion with one, Tracy called me, positive that they could not afford the purchase. They canceled the deal before they signed contracts. When pressed, she could not cite any evidence, only the ineffable feeling that she was spending too much. I had their balance sheet open on my computer screen; its numbers told a story of successful people living within their means. But Tracy was not only hosting the Pauper. She was a Homebody Buyer Personality, already very worried about everyone she was looking after in her house.

How wide is the gap between fearful Paupers and their reality? Tenured professors, the most job-secure people out there, worry about getting fired. Sensible, financially conservative retirees suddenly fear that they haven't factored in a 20–30% drop in the stock market. Wildly successful bankers with years of consistent bonuses talk themselves out of their all-cash purchases because *this is the year their luck runs out.* The same troll who compelled you to "stop throwing money away on rent" will invent these and other unlikely scenes. In the emotional swirl, you may forget what you have in your bank account. Or, in a simple turn of phrase, your $250,000 budget might turn into an unthinkably large "quarter of a million dollars." The distinction comes from fear, not prudence, and only raises the pressure.

Does money grow on trees, or not? Do you believe money is the root of all evil? How or when did your parents' money talk become your own? If you have never stopped to listen to your internal dialogue around your finances, you will want to start taking note of what it says. To avoid falling prey to the Pauper, I would recommend the following: Find the balance sheet you created in chapter 1 or complete it online (no judgment if you're only doing it for the first time). Then, using the link below or using its language from the appendix, create and sign an agreement with your spouse that will list three people to whom you will turn when the Pauper appears.† This trio could be a trusted friend, a professional mentor or advisor, and your real estate agent. Sign the agreement, and then share it, along with the balance sheet, with these three people. Let's hope cooler heads will prevail when they need to.

The Imposter

Some wish their houseguests didn't bring money fears with them. But be careful what you wish for. You could get something worse.

For the most part, I helped my music industry client Mo invest in brand-new condominium units he either rented out—or successfully flipped. This mission, though, was to find a new home for him and his fiancée. We locked onto a high-floor, three-bedroom apartment with sweeping views of the East River. It needed a new kitchen, but he didn't seem to mind. Two weeks after he signed contracts for the purchase, however, Mo called me, frantic about the condominium's

---

† Use a sample agreement at www.pursueyourhome.com/agreements.

application. "Scott, can they really ask me to provide reference letters? What the hell is going on?"

"Mo, it's nothing personal," I responded. "They ask this of anyone who wants to buy in their building. They just want to know their neighbors."

He was having none of it. "Scott, this is racist. I want out of this deal." I haven't mentioned yet that Mo is Black. I could tell this phone call wasn't getting him off the ledge. We met in person the next morning at his office.

I tiptoed into explaining how this entire condominium application process was a formality. All the building could do was either let him buy the apartment or buy it themselves at the same price. Really, the only actual bad news was that he had already signed the sales contract and there wasn't anything he could do to extract himself from the deal without losing his down payment. What was I missing?

His demeanor grew dark as he closed the door behind me and spoke in a hushed monotone. He gave me a window into his world, and some access into my naïve worldview too. He hated that plainclothes security still followed him around the high-end clothing stores in which he shopped. Residential buildings were more of the same. The suspicious looks from the concierge as he walked into a lobby, how women clutched their handbags in the elevator just a little more tightly, even the slight eyebrow raises from skeptical sales agents in new development galleries. And then he dropped the bomb. Mo feared that a decades-old run-in with the police would show up on his background check. He didn't want his fiancée, nor anyone in this condominium, to know about it.

He and his business partner had bought investment properties all over the country with loans that ran into the tens of millions. Fifteen years earlier, he had bought a small apartment in a cooperative building in Brooklyn too. Surely that board had done a rigorous review of his past. My read? The stakes were much higher now. Buying a home with his bride-to-be had put him in an unfamiliar, vulnerable, irrational state.

More than that, Mo was overcome with Imposter Syndrome. Here was someone at the peak of his professional powers, as financially successful as he'd ever been, frozen in fear that he would be found out as nothing more than a fraud.

I failed spectacularly at calming him down that day. Mo spent the next two months lashing out in every direction, especially mine. Yes, he finally got to the closing table, albeit with the same pained expression from that day we met in his office. And it was our last deal together. Less than a month later, he and his fiancée put the apartment back on the market—with another agent. They never moved in. He would never learn whether the Imposter's fears would transpire.

This falling-out got me thinking. I noted how little diversity there was in the composition of many condominium or cooperative communities I had visited across the city—except in their building staff. Is there discrimination happening in real estate? Unfortunately, yes, even in New York. I've seen egregious examples of racism, sexism, ageism, and antisemitism where you'd least expect it. In my heart, however, I didn't believe it was happening to Mo.

Racism is just one of many filters the Imposter might want to look through to make you feel unworthy. The further you travel out of your comfort zone, though, the more likely he will appear. High home prices in your market could be his cue to step onto the stage. Or being the first in your friend group to take the dive. Or just buying a house at all.

To be sure, you're going to have Imposter days. What can you do about this? Gather some facts to ground you, as a Meter Reader might. Get preapproved from a lender, if you haven't already, or look at your preapproval. That piece of paper will show you, in black and white, what you need to see: the purchase price at which someone is willing to lend you money. Then look at your balance sheet again. Let it remind you that your income is enough to make this happen, that you've saved enough. That you are enough.

And if you can, get introduced to homeowners in your market. Have coffee with them. Ask them to share their whole story of finding a home there. You are just a few years behind them. Like you, they are just trying to make a go of things in this crazy world. Homebuying probably made things crazier for them for a little while too.

The Grand Inquisitor

Alternatively, some buyers go down a different rabbit hole. Initially, Danny and Kristen just wanted to ascertain the structural integrity of a century-old house for which we had an accepted offer. Their houseguest, however, was just commencing a Torquemada-style Grand Inquisition.

Prior to their accepted offer, we had visited fifteen houses and made five bids. That's not the sign of a bargain hunter, but of a couple, in their early forties, on the heels of a long-awaited first marriage, eager to get on with their new life together. Yet Danny soon expressed misgivings about the price we had negotiated. His houseguest was the Dealmaker. Hers? The Grand Inquisitor.

Not everyone is worried about saving every last penny, even if Dealmakers do. For Kristen, the spotlight shifted over to trust. The Grand Inquisitor inside her believed this seller was hiding something, because it believed *everyone* was hiding something—and trying to pull one over on her. If trust issues are your Achilles' heel, they will be hypersensitized during your real estate transaction.

Night after night, I fielded torturous phone calls from Kristen's insistent houseguest. *Why won't they allow us more access to the house?*

Why is the attorney so slow to respond? Why can't they provide the paperwork we requested? What aren't they telling us? Nothing I said would halt this dogged determination to root out the heretic. For over six weeks, the attorneys went back and forth over legal minutiae, while the listing agent and I haggled over what items the seller would repair. How meaningless this all was, anyway. They were about to do a top-to-bottom renovation that would take at least two years!

Danny's Dealmaker tried to convert Kristen's Grand Inquisitor's mistrust into a $25,000 credit that ultimately cratered the negotiations. I winced three months later, when I saw that the house was sold to another buyer for a *million dollars more* than my clients' contract price. Her suspicious energy had kept her from their dream home.

Real estate agent Matt Kelly in Augusta, Georgia, helped his first-time buyer snag an underpriced $275,000 home. Before long, however, the Grand Inquisitor appeared too. The buyer could not be placated with the repairs a seller agreed to make. "I'm not buying someone else's BS," his client barked, unfazed by the seller's cooperation. He walked away over one wheelbarrow's worth of dirt left on the front lawn. Without a doubt, bailing out was easier when the earnest money deposit was only $4,000—and he even recovered that six months later from a sympathetic judge in small claims court. I doubt that buyer learned anything new from his aborted homebuying experience.

William was another client whose only faith was that every person involved in his purchase was either lying or withholding information. It made perfect sense; he was a retired police detective. How did it spiral out of control from there? More than once, he threatened to report the listing agent—an organized, calm, buttoned-up former kindergarten teacher, mind you—to the authorities for fraud. Thank goodness she was used to temper tantrums. This kind of vigilance works when chasing criminals, but less so when hunting houses. We held that deal together by a thread.

Retired police detectives aren't the only skeptical buyers. Bobbie and Rowan, for example, insisted on paying for the cost of a car and driver, something a New York City agent usually covers out of pocket for high-end buyer tours. While unspoken, it was clear they were guarding themselves from sales pressure tactics and guilt over a few hundred dollars that could have resulted in buying a multimillion-dollar apartment they didn't want. While logical on some level, this position comes with a cost of its own. Assuming someone will try to manipulate you embeds the entire relationship with mistrust and creates a barrier to connection. When you expect people to misbehave, are you encouraging them to be at their best?

To overcome your trust issues, reframe the questions you want to ask so they get to the heart of your concerns. *Why can't we get access?* could become *What specific things do we still want to see and analyze, and what is the risk in not knowing? Why is the attorney so slow to respond?* could become *It's annoying that the attorney is slow, but what is this really costing us? What aren't they telling us?* could become *Relax, that's just the Grand Inquisitor messing with my head.*

In real estate, there will be some degree of uncertainty. Stepping back and doing a little *what's-the-worst-thing-that-can-happen*-style analysis will unveil how much uncertainty you can live with, and how much is too much. And in unavoidably uncertain situations like these, it's imperative you're working with an agent you trust.

The Straight-A Student

Rather than mistrust the people on the other side of the transaction, this houseguest, the Straight-A Student, mistrusts what she doesn't know about the house *itself*, and what surrounds it. In truth, you've only spent a few minutes in a home for which you're about to fork over most of the money you have ever saved. And the questions come like a fire hose. *What if the neighbor does noisy work in his garage? What if the dog next door yips incessantly or the house creaks at night? What is the 10-year history of the property's real estate taxes? Is the building fiscally or structurally sound?* The Straight-A Student has no filter and only one gear to their data-collection mode: overdrive to get the "right answer."

They take notes during a showing, like that kid in the front row of class who writes down every word the teacher says. They shoot videos of the space, take photos of each kitchen faucet, bath fixture, and plaster molding. To get the "real scoop," they will study online reviews of the house builder and examine neighborhood rankings, walkability scores, and school ratings. And in the same way that Tripadvisor write-ups scare your spouse from committing to hotel after hotel, these houseguests will get themselves worked up over just about anything negative. I had clients who walked away from three fully negotiated deals because they could never get comfortable without "the complete picture." Like that bag of potato chips you can't stop eating, Straight-A Students will never know when to stop consuming information.

How do you keep your boundless desire for knowledge in check, then? For an apartment purchase, I would start by speaking to residents in the building. That may help calm your nerves. If you're buying a house, speak to friends who have bought one. What you'll quickly learn is that there is no such thing as perfect information. Perfect is not only the enemy of the good. It is, ironically, the enemy of your dream house.

You should also trust your agent to help prioritize which information, and how much of it, enables a good decision. Behavioral psychologist Herbert Simon called this *satisficing*, a portmanteau of *satisfy* and *suffice*. It's what most CEOs do, and why it's said that C students run the world. Because knowing everything on the test won't help your Straight-A Student pass this class. It may feel unnatural, but find a way to borrow some bravery. Ask yourself, *If I were a House Manager* (the most decisive Buyer Personality, you may recall), *what would I do?*

The Martyr

We all have that aunt who arrives an hour early for the family gathering, that cousin who turns every conversation into a political diatribe, or that sibling who has nothing nice to say about anyone. You have vast experience humoring your relatives' misbehavior. On the other hand, you may not be prepared at all for this houseguest, with her intolerable, poisonous comments. It is the Martyr who asks the most upsetting question of all: *Who are you to buy a home like this?*

There is an important distinction to be made between the Imposter and the Martyr. They both feel undeserving, but for different reasons. Mo's Imposter earlier in the chapter had forgotten the years of professional growth, the wins, and how much he had overcome. The Martyr's quandary lies in allowing the grace of good things to happen. Diligence has nothing to do with it. For example, Stephanie and Henry had just had their second child and were ready for a larger space. For most people, this would have been when they hit the eject button from living in New York City. Neither had high-salary careers—Stephanie worked as a high school administrator and Henry in a financial firm's back office. In their case, however, Stephanie's parents were willing to fund the entire purchase price as a gift. They would only have to cover the apartment's monthly charges.

Nearly one in four first-time homebuyers get help from family for their purchase today. But how would you react if, after years of being in the working world, you *still* needed this kind of financial assistance? Would you feel like everything you have ever worked for amounts to nothing? That somehow, in buying a home, the embodiment of accomplishment, you feel like you are putting your freedom, pride, or even your personal identity in peril?

We identified an apartment in an Upper East Side cooperative in which half of the dining room had already been converted into a third bedroom. It was priced well, too, because the seller's wife had recently died of cancer, and he could not bear to stay in the apartment any longer. Within a few days, the deal was negotiated. On the morning I expected them to sign contracts, I couldn't help but be enthusiastic. As I walked out onto the street from my apartment building to start my day, my cell phone rang. Stephanie's name popped up on the screen.

She and Henry were working through some tension and disagreement as to whether they could proceed. *Was the apartment too nice? Was the building too fancy? Would their kids somehow become spoiled?* She questioned whether they deserved the apartment if they couldn't afford to buy it on their own. The Martyr had emerged to ruin Stephanie and Henry's home search.

Before you judge them for being ungrateful, I left out one important detail. A dark cloud hung over what could have and should have been a happy day for Stephanie and Henry. I knew their angst ran deeper than worries about a financial gift because I had attended the funeral service for their first child a few years earlier. I will never forget Henry standing at the dais, sharing the heartbreaking grief of suddenly losing their three-year-old in a freak accident.

You might have lost your sibling or know someone who has. Is it that much of a reach to imagine the Martyr asking them why they weren't paying an appropriate penance for their blessings? These aren't just financial strings. They can be emotional strings, sewn directly onto your heart. So Stephanie wasn't encountering the typical last-minute, pre-signing jitters that required nothing more than an empathetic pat on the back and a "this is normal" pep talk.

What happened next I can only describe as an out-of-body experience. I stopped dead still on the sidewalk, and heard myself launch into a short, impassioned plea straight from the heart. I told Stephanie that she and Henry were an inspiration to hundreds, if not thousands, of people. They had lived through a tragedy, come out on the other side, and proved what is possible. They made our community and our world a more compassionate place. They didn't deserve to lose their son. But they absolutely deserved a home like this. This apartment would not just enable them to take their lives to the next level, but give them a platform to give back *more* to the world. That's why they found it. And I was put here to help them buy it.

Many people give, and give, and give some more, because they do not think they are worthy of receiving. They settle for less because the Martyr told them they weren't deserving of any of it. Can you allow good things to happen in your home search? Can you be grateful for life's countless ways of telling you how special you are? Can you accept the notion that whatever good you put into the world must return to you? You deserve a home that you love. Everyone does. Don't let anyone, especially the Martyr, tell you otherwise.

How should you manage this houseguest? Surround yourself with friends and family with whom you can safely share any feelings of inadequacy. You don't want "bless your heart," but "I know exactly how you are feeling. I've been there too." This is the difference between sympathy and empathy. You need the latter.

More importantly, don't share your homebuying wins, big or small, except with those who you know will celebrate without any reservation. Identify these people in advance, as they are likely to be a subset of even that group you trust to hold your hand during the home search's most intense periods.

Draw from the wisdom of the gag order around pregnancy, which couples often deploy. Many expecting parents are reluctant to share their good news too soon, or at all. Their thinking: *What happens if there's a miscarriage?* Or, *Why should we upset our friend Missy who has been unsuccessfully trying to get pregnant?* It's a minefield of calamities that could lead anyone to white-knuckle the first trimester, and perhaps the second, without a peep.

This explains why your friends won't share about their home purchase until they've closed. It's not that you're a bad friend. They just didn't cement their circle of trust before they got lost in their house drama. Don't take it personally.

The Arsonist

If you look closely, you will see where your own actions had an impact on any unhappy real estate results so far, just as they have in other areas of your life. But don't forget that most buyers are in this together with a partner. And for all the attempts to sabotage yourself, it's that much more heartbreaking when you or your spouse undertakes to destroy a deal for the other person. If this journey were a horror movie, the call would be coming from inside the house. The Arsonist takes extreme measures to burn it down before you buy it.

I had the sense that Tina didn't want to move, but she never said anything specific to me or her husband, Darren, as they signed contracts, got their mortgage, and submitted the application to the cooperative's board. She waited until their co-op board interview, the last step before getting approval to close, to get the fire going. Her husband was stunned when she got up, said, "I'm sorry, I just can't take this," then walked out in the middle of the meeting. Buyers who so obviously try to get a board to reject them could expect to get nothing back from their down payment. Yet these buyers spent three years, and a lot of legal fees, litigating over it. The Arsonist made quite a commitment to ensuring that they didn't purchase that apartment.

Other Arsonists are less extreme, but more insidious. Jeffrey never joined his wife, Sheryl, on any tours and went so far as to let her submit offers on properties, two of which were accepted. He had the excuse that he was traveling for work, but really, he was operating in bad faith. Each time they came close to a deal, he had their attorney insert language that worked like a poison pill. It guaranteed that the seller would not proceed. In due course, Sheryl came to understand that he had zero interest in moving from their New Jersey home. She had been spinning her wheels.

As a buyer, you could find yourself on the receiving end of the Arsonist. I heard about a couple who were ready to leave New York City after the pandemic. In preparation for the move, the wife took a new job in Miami and they listed their brownstone. As the closing neared, however, the husband announced he was staying in the house and wanted a divorce. The buyers, who had already contracted to purchase the home, were more than a little miffed. They had to decide whether to litigate and try to force the sale, or walk away. The wife of the selling couple didn't stick around for the fireworks. She had a matrimonial attorney and a relocation to manage.

It is worth taking a pause in your home search if any of this feels familiar. You may want to carefully contemplate the fissures in your relationship, or factor in how well or how poorly each of you communicates. Otherwise, you might be hiring legal counsel for a divorce instead of a purchase.

The Mythologist

The bruises accumulate and you will suffer from a little real estate fatigue, whether the housing market you're in is hot or not. And that's when the Mythologist reports for duty, after every other houseguest has already filed in and taken great pains to gum up the works.

You might know a guy who can't stop talking about the missed opportunity to invest in a company that reached unicorn status. I am sure you have a friend who regrets letting go of that woman or man who *would have changed everything*. This fallacy permeates the real estate search too. The Mythologist never wants you to forget The One That Got Away.

Over the years, I have encountered many New Yorkers who gave up on buying after a few tries. It seemed like each one had a property that slipped through their fingers. There were stories like these: "My landlord wanted to sell my rental apartment to me for $85,000—I was insane to have passed that up," or "I had a chance to buy at the bottom of the market in 1991," or "There was this screaming deal I passed on right after 9/11. . . ."

You will lose out on a house here or there. And it stings, especially when it seemed like you were *so close*, and later, when you start to believe the wound was self-inflicted. But the longer you wait to get back in the game, the worse it gets. Otherwise, the Mythologist will overwhelm you with nostalgia. Combining the Greek word *nostos*, coming home, with the word *alga*, pain, it could just as easily be translated as homesickness. To put a finer point on it, and to get at what I think its true meaning is, nostalgia is grieving for a home that *never was*. It's that mythical quality that makes slipping into nostalgia so potentially toxic here.

Be wary when you start ruminating over what you could have done differently. That energy will only push you in the wrong direction. Ask yourself: What *really* happened? What is there to be learned? It is possible that in examining things at a distance, you might see things in a new light. Maybe you would have outgrown that place in a year. Worse yet, you might have been stuck trying to sell it in next year's down market. Trust that it is all for the best, that right now is exactly when you are meant to find your dream home.

Unpack Your Real Estate Baggage

Let us return to our 13th-century medieval poet. Rumi knew that you would loathe your inner houseguests' unsolicited advice, their well-placed barbs, their predictions of loss, and their paranoia. There is a gravity to all this undermining inner monologue. Ben Franklin commented that guests, like fish, go bad after three days. Is it fair to say that some of your visitors have been living rent-free in your head for much longer, even most of your life? And unlike your actual friends and relatives, how much power do you have in asking these houseguests to leave?

Your home search serves, in part, to put all your glorious imperfections on display. You will come face-to-face with your greed, anger, defensiveness, and mistrust. You will brush up against your restlessness and dread. You will meet the apprehensive younger version of yourself with a less expansive viewpoint. These are the perils of being human, and the allergic reactions to change. You're contending with a structure older than any man-made building anywhere in the world—your brain—that's also your toughest enemy. Did you ever think that your house search could be a personal growth program as well? It is, whether you like it or not.

As unenthusiastic about recognizing these parts of yourself as you might be, have compassion for your guests. Rumi begs us to "meet them at the door laughing, and invite them in . . . because each has been sent as a guide from beyond." I would recommend you go even further. Bless your mess. Be grateful for it. You have armed yourself with two things you didn't have before your house search began: information and awareness. One gives you a clearer sense of what you would love in a home, the other a visceral understanding and honest assessment of how you get in the way of your own happiness.

You don't have to be ashamed of your houseguests, even if you, as the host, wish you could give them Airbnb-style one-star reviews. How vastly improved would things be if you told the people in your life you felt anxious, rather than acting out the role of the Imposter, the Pauper, or the Martyr? In calling these characters out, you defang them, and you take away their hold over you. You're less likely to act out on what they say.

Isn't it worth unpacking your emotional baggage, then? As I've said again and again, communication replaces fear and doubt with trust and builds stronger relationships. As you candidly share how you are feeling, you trust yourself more. With a knowledge of what you want, appreciation for your old, automatic reactions, and a willingness to share both, you will access new ways of finding your home, and won't have to rely on the voices of your past any longer.

CHAPTER 6

Make Your Own
Housing Market

The Easiest Way to
Find Your Home

"The place in which I'll fit will
not exist until I make it."
—James Baldwin

Home, Grown

Your mental houseguests—and they really have gone mental, haven't they?—have left quite a mess in their wake. Are you going to let them waste any more valuable time and energy making you worry about what could go wrong with the next opportunity? What if I told you that you could delegate all the practical concerns of your real estate deal to your agent instead, and then almost forget about them? That would take a lot off your plate, wouldn't it?

The clients in chapter 5 amply demonstrated to you that the transaction is only the tip of the iceberg. This chapter will take that notion further, and show you why giving up control of your real estate journey is the smartest move you can make. Because there is a bigger insight you will need all your energy and focus to embrace: By building your faith in what you cannot see, your dream house will start looking for *you*.

🏠 🏠 🏠

Until then, bringing the dream house part of the American Dream to life will still feel like a heavy lift. Your mood swings with every headline. In the face of the pressure to "do something," you impatiently text your agent and hit refresh on that listings website multiple times a day. And why would real estate be tough to master? Everyone has become an expert in everything else, haven't they? So you heed the call to *do your own research*. You turn to Reddit, Facebook, YouTube, podcasts, and maybe some less credible sources of information, if they exist. Your research turns up all manner of potential real estate misbehavior and opens up more questions than answers about the transaction, not to mention dialed-up feelings of doubt and mistrust.

How's this approach working out? We head to the sidelines because a convincing talk-show or podcast host said mortgage rates are too high, inventory is too low, or the stock market faces the prospect of uneven performance. Then we follow the herd when enough headlines report a few signs of recovery. Housing markets rise and fall on the popularity of easy-to-digest explanations for where we are in the market cycle. They have a seductive allure that transcends budget. Does their digestibility make them any more accurate? Hardly.

The financial markets make my point even more clearly. Over the last 20 years, not even the world's most famous investor—Warren Buffett—outperformed the stock market. He doesn't have high hopes for your investment prowess either. He recommends that you buy an index fund, the same boring investment vehicle that handily beat him, rather than be reckless with your savings. So would I.

I surmise that your research has left you worse than empty-handed. For all you may have learned, something is still missing. It will take more than a purchase and sale every seven to ten years, more than binge-watching HGTV, and more than a few hours of googling. It will take more than even this book to get there.

You can put every factoid, anecdote, or data point you have gathered under the header *Seeing is Believing*, and set it aside for a moment. I'll let you in on the secret: Stop trying to beat the housing market you can see. You are overcomplicating things.

You Make Your Own Market

You have hired an agent with whom you can communicate. You have enough sense of what homes in your area are supposed to cost. You have already gone through the process of knowing what you want by seeing what you don't. You have a sense of what you love. You have even unpacked your emotional baggage. I submit to you that there is nothing left to write down or figure out.

Step back and meditate on this: What most would define as the "housing market" is a swirl of competing forces, unknowable in their totality. No one can capture more than a sliver of what is going on. If you were to zoom in enough, the market you're trying to time or understand disintegrates. There's no market out there you'll ever be able to master. There is just what's inside of you. So the real choice is to either press on productively or keep looking for answers that aren't likely to help and, more likely, will hold you back.

Most instinctively choose to keep rooting around for answers in the past. A study by Queen's University in Canada tracked thought patterns using fMRI scans and estimated that people have approximately 6,200 thoughts per day, most of which are what they call "thought worms." You need not be Sherlock Holmes to deduce that most of these repetitive thoughts are going to be negative, and other research affirms this intuition. As we discussed in chapter 4, the human brain is inclined to focus on negative experiences of the past to make sense of the world and your survival. Yet here's the rub, spelled out by author and business coach Lewis Howes. He wrote, "When your body and mind are both living in the past, then your thoughts and emotions are rooted in negativity and *impossibility*" (my emphasis).

Yes, it goes against our instincts to focus on the future. We complain about what hasn't happened rather than consider that it just hasn't happened *yet*. One pesky word, a world of difference. It was Henry Ford who said, "Whether you think you can or think you can't—you're right." And he is accurate: You can decide that seeing is believing or you can flip the script, and decide that *believing is seeing*. Taking the latter path requires a leap of faith: believing that **you make your own market**. You and your agent have Activated and Aligned your property magnet. I am asking you to commit to your vision of your dream house and stop worrying about how it will come together.

I confess that I cannot quite explain how it works, but I can explain how to tap in to the magic of The Magnetic Method. Put step 3 into practice: Amplify the strength of your vision. Clear the path for it. Surround it with positive thoughts. Daydream about it. Share it. What I am describing is ridding yourself altogether of the idea that seeing is believing. Forget the number of bedrooms, or the exact location, or the style of home, or really, anything physical about the house.

In chapter 2, I suggested you create a vision board. You may not have done it. Or, if you did, you haven't looked at it in a while. Either way, you may find that you want to redo it using all you have learned since, and look at it each morning. Filmmaker, speaker, and content creator Prince EA explains what happens when you do. In his motivational video on the power of dreams, watched more than 12 million times on YouTube, he also challenges conventional wisdom. "Martin Luther King didn't have a dream," he said. "His dream had him." Why not let your vision have you? Every minute you spend strengthening its pull on you is worthwhile.

What does committing to your vision look like in practice? It resembles someone like Thomas Edison, the American archetype of persistence. What drove him to press on, day after day, until his most famous invention was a reality, was a rock-solid commitment to his vision. He delegated everything else to his "muckers"—a revolving door of industrious assistants—to make room for inspiration. Edison had already decided the light bulb would come to fruition while the world still read books by candlelight. The passion of his commitment carried him through the 10,000 attempts it took to be successful. I am certain you won't need to see that many houses to find yours.

Even so, you should definitely delegate anything that feels like work to your agent.

⌂ ⌂ ⌂

The impact of commitment like this cannot be overstated. Scottish mountaineer and writer W. H. Murray explained how this works: "The moment one definitely commits oneself, then Providence moves too. All sorts of things occur to help one that would never otherwise have occurred. A whole stream of events issue from the decision, raising in one's favor all manner of unforeseen incidents and assistance, which no one could have dreamt would come [their] way." How I translate that: Committing to a vision is a power move that allows you to both let go of control of the outcome and make room for miracles.

I was two years into my real estate career and newly engaged when the unforeseen stepped in and showed me the miraculous power of commitment to a vision. In my case, the vision was getting married and creating a life together. One summer afternoon, my fiancée (now wife of nearly two decades as of the time of this writing) and I were scheduled to tour a potential wedding venue. I had a half hour to get there, so I walked from Tribeca, where I was, to the Lower East Side, where she would meet me. Leaning against a dumpster I passed was a piece of pressed tin removed from the ceiling of a nearby loft. This piece looked like a frame, its blank, flat, rectangular center surrounded with a three-inch band of curlicues, covered in flaking white paint. I had never seen one up close and was struck by its beautiful detail. So, before I marched on, I tucked it under my arm.

The piece's sharp edges began digging into my skin before I got to the end of the block. As I crossed Broadway, however, I spotted the solution—a luggage shop that I must have passed blindly for years. A minute later, the salesperson handed me a thick, clear, plastic suitcase bag, with which I wrapped my unusual acquisition.

I hustled by the ducks and chickens hanging in shop windows, whizzed past the fish on ice, and walked through the horizontal park that separates Chinatown from the Lower East Side. Veering onto Orchard Street, I noticed a bright red storefront, oddly stuck between a run-down deli and an office supply store. It was a gallery, but like nothing I had seen before. Portraits were everywhere, and each one painted on an unusual surface. A face on what had been an old children's chalkboard. A Goth couple re-created on a book cover. A repurposed, oval-shaped standing mirror showcased a mysterious woman staring back at me instead of my reflection. I was transfixed.

"What's that you got there?" boomed a voice from the back of the store. I had completely forgotten what I was carrying under my arm. The shop owner—also the artist—introduced himself as Zito and asked me what I wanted to do with the tin. He had no idea how random it was that I was even standing there, and I told him I had no idea what I wanted.

He was unfazed. "Sometimes I paint portraits not of people as they are today, but when they were kids." I recalled a faded photograph my fiancée kept on her refrigerator. It was from her sixth birthday party, posing with one hand on her hip and one behind her head. It made me smile whenever I walked into her kitchen. We briefly discussed his prices, and I agreed to leave the tin in his gallery so I could "think about it." But I already had my answer.

How strange it all was. Over the course of a one-mile walk, I had found the medium, commandeered a carrying case for it, and found the artist to work with it and paint a beautiful engagement gift. How could I not see this as the culmination of some cosmic connectedness? It still hangs on our wall 20 years later.

In real estate, I have also experienced far too much not to believe in the unseen. An impromptu afternoon walk with a buyer that turned into a seven-million-dollar sale. A cold call to a classified ad that resulted in thirty million dollars of transactions. A property we overpriced so egregiously that it got press coverage—and found a buyer in a week.

I once found a buyer for a stale two-bedroom listing I couldn't otherwise give away as I walked out of a cocktail party. And not only that, the cooperative board in that building, who had a strict no-pet policy, approved his dog.

Deals that died untimely deaths were resurrected months later. One property that didn't sell became available again just as the next-door neighbor passed away—offering an opportunity to combine two units at an unheard-of low price. This miracle gave my wife and me the room we needed for our third child. So intensify and Amplify your vision. Then the magic will happen for you too.

Home Delivery

The next step to making your own real estate market? Believing that your property is out there. As the signs say along the highway, you could be home now. Know that success is assured. Stop worrying about how it's going to happen. In the parlance of the hero's journey, it is the *approach*. It is the gathering of all your skills and forces at your disposal to do battle with your biggest enemies: doubt and fear. It requires the utmost faith that you have what it takes.

In that spirit, I recommend you abandon house hunting and opt for Home Delivery, where the universe, in partnership with your team, can be your real estate scout. In other words, let your house find you. I'm reluctant to call it manifesting, but that's how the Oxford online dictionary defines the word *manifest*: "clear or obvious to the eye." Our system makes your home so obvious that you just need to reach out and grab it. This is the fourth and last step of The Magnetic Method: Attract.

Act with the curiosity, innocence, imagination, and belief of young children, what Buddhists call a beginner's mind. We all had these qualities once. Why can't anything be possible again? With this attitude, you might spot a property online that is completely different from what you set out to buy, in a different style or location. You suddenly think of a person to call, or you decide to take a drive down a random street. You stop to speak to someone standing in front of their house who tells you they've been thinking of selling just that very morning. Maybe your cousin's acquaintance mentions something in church about a listing, or your friends just "thought of you" when they heard about a property coming to market. Your agent might have an out-of-the-box idea for you. You will do less work, but must pay closer attention, because your house is being pulled to you like a magnet.

Phil is a great example. He flew into New York to find a *pied-à-terre*, a part-time or second home literally translated as a "foot on the ground." But it became obvious during our property tour that we needed to adjust either his price range, his location, or the types of buildings he regarded as acceptable. Over coffee, I learned that he was open to any area that gave him a taste of the bustle of the city. Moreover, Phil only intended this home to be for his personal use, so he didn't need a building with a policy friendly to investors who plan to rent out their properties. Before we even stood up, I thought of a building on the other side of town that ticked all the boxes, and had two available units. He closed three months later on one of them, getting everything he wanted—at 20% below his original budget.

Alice was a wealthy out-of-town rental client who also let go of control and let her house find her. I trusted my intuition, and recommended a SoHo unit that cost 50% more than what she said she wanted to spend. It just seemed like the right move for some reason. I could see as soon as we walked in the door that I had been smart to trust my gut. Although we ran all around town for another day at her insistence, she had already found her house. Later, she told me that using the apartment to entertain clients had helped her grow her business tenfold in less than two years. It was *so* much her house that she even bought it a few years later from the landlord.

Once you have committed, and stepped up your faith in the process, nothing can stop the magic of Home Delivery, not even a global pandemic. While prices skyrocketed in nearly every other region and city in America, the housing market in the five boroughs stalled out on March 16, 2020, when property showings became illegal. No one was allowed to visit apartments at all during the three-month lockdown that followed. Some New Yorkers escaped to a second home or a short-term rental outside the city. Over a million young professionals broke their leases and moved in with family across the country. Everyone in New York City was cooped up in their apartments.

Bill and Pamela had been browsing open houses for a few months as COVID-19 struck. A few weeks into the shutdown, I saw a massive price reduction on one property in their search area. When I sent it to them, they called me back almost immediately. They had looked at it in person nearly a year earlier, before we started working together. And while they could not see it again in person, neither could anyone else. Without any competition, we negotiated what my colleagues have since dubbed a "COVID deal." Bill and Pamela had no better option than to employ Home Delivery. They look like geniuses for doing so.

Every real estate agent across the country whom I interviewed for this book has at least one story that goes like this: The buyer was about to give up, and the agent reassured them that if they just had some faith, a house would materialize. And then it *would*, on cue, within a week or so! One Kentucky agent sheepishly confessed that he, too, needed to have a bit more faith, in a market that wasn't producing much inventory. But after a heart-to-heart with his buyer, during which he recommitted to the search, he found not one, but *two* brand-new houses located side by side for both this buyer and another as well. Home Delivery worked so well that two strangers stood in a communal driveway, face-to-face, and negotiated how they would share use of it. They each signed purchase contracts on the spot.

Occasionally, the house may find you directly, rather than land in your agent's lap. Lisa Weissman, a highly successful agent in Westchester County, home to many of New York City's bedroom communities, shared with me that she had nearly given up on an executive who had dismissed numerous houses over many months. She herself had seen, then pooh-poohed, a new-to-market house that she didn't feel was good enough for him, primarily because it backed up to train tracks. He saw it, too, then called her about it. "Why didn't you send this to me?" he asked. She knew his son had autism, but couldn't have known that he also loves trains. Now he sits in delight, watching the Metro-North go by. Her usefulness as his agent in this case? To build *his* faith that this was possible, so he could pounce when the right house appeared.

⌂ ⌂ ⌂

For some buyers, this kind of faith is nearly impossible to come by. You may recall Leslie and Stewart in chapter 2, self-proclaimed permanent renters who had sworn off buying. In particular, Stewart couldn't stop bad-mouthing the real estate industry during our intake call. Tiring of this negativity, and nearly ready to pull the plug, I trotted out a Hail Mary play I sometimes use to shake things up. "Okay. One more thing. What does 'home' mean to you?"

Through the phone, I heard the creak of the chair as Stewart leaned back. He sighed, then answered, "Home is the people I'm around." Leslie agreed. "Our community is more important than anything." The question had magically moved our conversation from the complaints of the past to the realities of the present. Leslie was "bummed not to have the kitchen that I want" in their city rental. And in a vulnerable moment, Stewart confessed that he was heart-broken that his landlord might sell their apartment the following year. We got off the phone and I didn't think anything more of it.

Not two months later, I ran into Stewart at an event. "Scott, you're not going to believe what happened," he said. The agent who had found them their rental apartment more than a decade earlier had called them the day after we had spoken, and offered them a gorgeous, renovated off-market four-bedroom apartment to buy, at an amazing price. And soon after, they became Manhattan homeowners.

Had our phone call been the inspiration they needed to look away from the past, and into the future? They finally divulged in some roundabout way that they were ready for more. As soon as they did, their dream home miraculously appeared.

Diplomatic advisor Tal Becker, involved in some of the thorn-iest negotiations in the Middle East, described the intermediary as one who must believe in "the permanent possibility of the presently unimaginable." Real estate agents have the same role, just a different goal in mind. When you tell me you want to make this idea of a new home a reality, it's already real to me. It is an inevitability. I don't know exactly what the house will look like, or how it will happen, but I have no doubt that we will find it. An agent's conviction could be the single most important quality they have, though maintaining it requires ongoing effort for anyone involved. Trust that you can lean on your agent's faith in you. It's sure to be a little steadier.

An even older text than the Bible, the *I Ching*, spoke of the power of faith four millennia ago. "Waiting is not mere empty hoping. It has the inner certainty of reaching the goal"—the Chinese had the benefit of the bamboo around them to inspire this insight. Bamboo will grow, in stealth mode, for months, or even years. Only when it emerges from the ground do you realize how much work its root stalks, or *rhizomes*, have already done. Over a 60-day spurt, a huge patch of bamboo might grow more than two feet a day.

"Doing nothing," therefore, is not necessarily doing nothing. It can be an empowered choice to be patient, to nurture your intuition, and to strengthen your awareness so you know when the right home has arrived. This is a refinement of the messages you received at the end of chapter 3 about whom to hire and whom to trust with your then-shaky vision. These messages soon appear like a bolt of lightning, or a tingly physical sensation, or a neon sign. Or an agent willing to tell you that you need to pause your search and save more money for a down payment. Would you be open to hearing *that* message, that you need to take one step back to take two steps forward?

Some clients seem to ignore all my communications, challenging or encouraging. Others only appear to ignore them. Alyssa, for example, was very skilled at listening for the Home Delivery alert. For about four months, I regularly sent her curated lists of properties that I thought would be of interest, at least a few every other week, to no response. That is, until she wrote back to one email, "This is the one. Let's go buy it." I kept the faith that one of my ideas would work. She waited for the right one to appear. She didn't second-guess the yes.

Remember Jane and Brian in chapter 3, who I thought wanted to fire me? They had asked me to email them every day, either with new listings we liked, with properties we reviewed and already tagged as a bad fit, or with a confirmation that there was nothing new on the market that day. A month into our daily back-and-forth, Jane finally leaned in to the patience that Home Delivery required of her. "You already know the kind of building I'd like to be in. I'm more on board now with waiting for the right one and not rushing into finding a place before growing our family."

They remembered why they were looking for a new home. There's much more at stake than just finding a house. Emerson wrote about it 150 years ago on the last page of his groundbreaking 1836 essay, *Nature*: "Every spirit builds itself a house; and beyond its house, a world; and beyond its world a heaven. Know then, that the world exists for you: build, therefore, your own world." As I have said, you make your own market. Another way to put it: You make your own magnet. And on some fundamental level, you *are* the magnet.

> You make your own market.
> You make your own magnet.
> In essence, you are the magnet.

🏠 🏠 🏠

I know this philosophy bumps up against the rough-and-tumble world of real estate. At one time or another, you may have been taught that the only way to reign supreme in a real estate negotiation is by being tough, by playing your cards close to the vest, by never splitting the difference. I get it. But this is where Home Delivery has even more to offer you. This attitude elevates and expands the range of actions you can take. You can more patiently wait for the right home to appear.

You don't have to suffer through any part of homebuying. It can be far more fun and enjoyable. For the most part, anyway.

Try this on for size: You're not competing against other buyers. And as your representative, I'm not competing against the agents on the other side of the transaction. Together, we are not trying to pull one over on anyone, take advantage, or beat anyone at the game. I go after houses on behalf of my clients with as much vigor as any agent might. But I think about infusing every aspect of the negotiation with kindness.

Kindness may feel like a dirty word, or a sign of weakness, but it is anything but. Kindness is setting boundaries with tough love, while holding you and others more accountable. Kindness requires asking clarifying questions. Kindness results in wasting less time on misunderstandings. Kindness is firmness, and is more effective when the unpleasant conversations inevitably take place. I'm a huge fan of kindness. When you embrace this kind of kindness, you will occasionally be uncomfortable. But it's only temporary, especially compared to the long-lasting enjoyment of your forever home.

No one is perfect in a transaction. Kindness is an ideal I have not always achieved. But does what I have described seem like weakness to you? Roughly two billion dollars of real estate sales later, I would say no. Given how many on the other side of my real estate negotiations end up hiring me years later, it stands to reason that we are doing something very right. Do you know what is weak, though? Being *nice*. Nice is as awful as any other four-letter word. Nice is me telling you what you want to hear. Nice is pretending everything is fine when it isn't. Nice is going along to get along. Nice is being afraid to ruffle feathers. Nice is dancing around the elephant in the room. Nice is smiling when you don't mean it. Don't be nice. And don't hire nice agents. Nice agents finish last. Nice is a mostly unproductive addition to your home search, even though a smile now and then will go a long way.

I have toiled to keep money out of the spotlight in this book. After all, you won't snuggle up with your deal, nor will it keep you warm at night. Still, money has been lurking beneath the floorboards, just waiting for that moment to distract from what will help make your dreams come true. And there will be plenty of these distractions, the closer you get to your closing, as you'll soon see.

Happily, however, embracing Home Delivery, and its requirement to level up your faith in the process, has an interesting way of making negotiations to secure your home much easier. Ray Dalio, the founder of Bridgewater Associates, the largest hedge fund in history at the time of this writing, agrees in his book *Principles*. He proposes that "the quest for business excellence and the search for personal realization need not be mutually exclusive—and can, in fact, be essential to each other. This is the summary of the win-win situation." You can reconcile your emotional desires with the financial realities inherent in buying a home. I am certain you will catch many more deals with honey than with vinegar. I know my clients have. When the line between winning and losing your real estate deal is so small, every kind word and every extra second of listening could be the deciding factor. It's a game of square inches, not square feet. So play the game with extreme care.

Making your own market flows from the combination of commitment, faith, patience, intuition, and communication. It may feel strange and counterintuitive for a while. But I promise that it will hold together through whatever ups and downs remain and get you to the closing table in one piece. Even better, you are almost there! You only have to take one more demanding detour on the way home.

CHAPTER 7

House Training

Homebuying's Hardest Lessons

"*The home is not the one tame place in a world of adventure; it is the one wild place in a world of rules and set tasks.*"
—G. K. Chesterton

It's Getting Hot in Here

You have made it through so much of your journey already, with all of its false starts, dramatic pauses, valiant sword fights, and epic internal battles. You waited as patiently as you could, maybe less patiently than you hoped, but it's all good, right? You found your house! You just need to get from here to the closing table. What else could possibly go wrong?

I know I said you should let your real estate agent do the remaining work for you and let your intuition and faith guide you the rest of the way home. Well, that's not entirely possible, because there's a little more internal interference you're likely to encounter.

You see, it was never just about a new house. You are on the brink of becoming someone new, and your old sense of self is in jeopardy of being lost. Bob Proctor, among the old guard of the self-help movement, offers a house-oriented analogy. He writes that "the self-image operates like the thermostat in your home. Once your image is set, your life is on course to produce the physical manifestation of the mental image you hold." A temperature-controlled life, however, is impossible to maintain in the final throes of your house hunt. Yet we remain a confederacy of comfort seekers. You thought those house-guests in chapter 5 were annoying? Get ready to face off with the real estate scenarios you fear the most and that hit even closer to home. The universe conspires to create an inner housing crisis made just for you, an ordeal full of horrible behavior, nasty people, and unexpected drama, wherein you must agree to a spiritual transaction before the financial one. By hook or by crook, your house has more to teach you, until you learn what this journey was meant for. The main lesson? You often have to lose yourself to gain your dream home.

Demolition Day

Sometimes your house wants to rough *you* up, or show you you're not as tough as you think you are. Amy and her husband, Paul, found a high-floor apartment that came with two balconies, a river view, glorious sunsets, and only one pesky requirement—a full renovation. The week they were scheduled to close, however, there was a flood in one of the bedrooms that required immediate repair. Don't want to believe that the universe has a sense of humor? Amy was a highly successful tort attorney who brought asbestos class action suits together, and in the irony of all ironies, when the sellers pulled up the wooden parquet tiles, asbestos was found in the floor glue. No one was aware of its health risks better than she. These buyers were unexpectedly at a crossroads. Would they look for a way out? Or would they put her years of asbestos litigation expertise to the side and look for a solution?

Dilemmas like this are almost guaranteed to happen in real estate. Go down one road, and you will wade through additional inspections, pained conversations, requests for credits, and contentious bickering. Go down the other road—that is, walk away—and you might second-guess things for the rest of your life. Think of it like a compressed version of the four stages of grief, even though the house isn't necessarily gone! You'll go into shock. "This can't be happening!" (stage 1: Denial). Then you'll start to blame others for the predicament (stage 2: Anger). Then you'll try to reopen negotiations, even though money won't get to the heart of it (stage 3: Bargaining). Then, when you've stopped spinning, you'll be right back where you started, and *still* not be happy about it (stage 4: Depression).

Amy and Paul had their moments when they were *this close* to walking away. And I suspect that her professional experience making veiled threats, which I had to sheepishly convey to the seller side, only made things worse. In the end, the sellers completed the asbestos remediation work themselves, grumbling all the way to the closing table. As an agent, there was little to do but listen and let everyone vent. I'll describe the entire closing process and its potential pitfalls in the next chapter.

♠ ♠ ♠

The world can be pretty anxiety-provoking these days. If you have a tendency to worry, your house—and the universe—might escalate things to the breaking point in order to show you what you're made of. An agent I met recently told me about a couple with a $500,000 budget who finally found a house after 18 months—but continued to fret over everything that could go wrong. It probably didn't help that the wife was having a baby two weeks before the scheduled closing! On the last day the buyers could terminate the contract during the review period, the wife went bananas. How were they going to choreograph this closing with a newborn? How were they going to afford any overlap between selling their home and buying the new one? What if either home didn't close? They could be holding two houses, or could be homeless.

All of this had already been discussed *ad nauseam*. The buyers could not have missed exactly what they would be in for. The closing was always happening right before the purchase. The baby's due date had not changed either. They had just woken up to the morass that they themselves had created by setting plans in motion to buy this house. Think of it like one extended demolition day, except the contracting crew is taking its sledgehammers not to the walls and countertops, but to your daily life.

The agent calmly reassured them that the price they were paying was almost 10% below market value, and there hadn't been a deal like this in over three years in their market. He also reminded them their buyer was paying cash for their house, and that the new house was the only one they had ever felt good about. Most importantly, he showed them how he could "make it effortless" for them: He coordinated and hired an "army of high schoolers" to pack the house they were selling. He also confirmed that the new mortgage's first payments would not begin for more than a month after the closing (NOTE: the "meter" doesn't start running on mortgage interest until the closing day, though a bank will often collect a specific amount of prepaid interest at the closing). And he helped them get access to peace of mind, in the form of a potential bridge loan to cover any surprise out-of-pocket closing expenses. In the end, the buyers survived the last-minute stress without pulling the rip cord. They became first-time parents, first-time homeowners, and came out with a little more maturity.

🏠 🏠 🏠

These final steps toward your new house will ultimately quiet any doubts you have about the direction of your life. Bear this in mind, however: The universe will make them much louder first.

On our pre-tour consult call, Gina joked, "When we go to look at apartments, Scott, do not show me anything with a view of New Jersey. I never want to see it again." After more than 10 years so close, yet so far away, in the suburbs of the state next door, she and her husband, Neil, could not wait to get back to New York City. They sold their suburban house in midsummer, jubilantly crossed the George Washington Bridge in their beat-up SUV, and settled into a four-bedroom rental apartment near their children's school. Their expectation was that they would find a permanent home within the year. But between their jobs and settling into new routines, that deadline whizzed past. To be fair, we had been looking at properties, and Neil and Gina had even bid on one. They never stopped telling me how much they loved their rental, though. It had everything they were looking for.

They had lived there for nearly two years when their landlord, whom we'll call Ron, broached the subject of selling the apartment to them. This was always a possibility; he had only become a landlord because the apartment had not sold in a slower market, and he could not afford to keep it empty.

The timing of his offer wasn't unexpected, however. I had just seen the certified letter the property management company had sent to Neil and Gina, explaining why they wouldn't be permitted to rent for a third year. Later, they would claim that, in their fog, they didn't grasp that anything was wrong, and why would they? They paid their rent punctually and the landlord seemed happy to have them. The catch? The letter pointed out that when the original 12-month lease had ended, he had never provided the co-op a copy of a lease renewal.

Ron's logic: Without a formal renewal, he could get away without paying the fees the building levied on those owners who became landlords. The co-op's logic: We have rules. And they had just caught on that he was thousands of dollars behind in unpaid fees. My clients' dilemma: to move out, which they were not at all interested in, or to further involve themselves with someone so obviously ethically confused. They asked me to handle the transaction, and I offered them some advice: Don't do it. Don't steer straight into this hurricane. But it was there in its eye, they insisted, where they saw their dream home.

I took cold comfort that the lease had laid out the basics of this possible sale. The tenants had a right of first refusal should someone else offer to buy the apartment. The landlord's leasing agents had also made sure to include the commission rate at which his firm and mine would be paid if the tenants bought the apartment, another common practice. None of this proved helpful, though. After the sale price had been negotiated, Ron, in his parallel universe where rules didn't apply, determined he did not owe a brokerage commission to his agent, to my firm, or to anyone.

To be clear, I'm not saying that this was logical, nor that Ron wouldn't eventually have to cave. But I've seen how slow the wheels of justice turn, and I wasn't sure Neil and Gina had the stomach to wait it out. They were clearly passionate about staying put, but they also panicked and had me show them other options to buy and rent. Things were coming to a boiling point, because neither firm was going to walk away from their brokerage commission if they chose to stay.

In the last chapter, I wrote about how kindness has helped my clients buy and sell a great deal of property. I must confess my inclination here was to shove kindness to the side. On one call with Neil and Gina, I laid out all the ways they could stoop to Ron's level. (1) They could report to the building's board that he had installed an illegal Jacuzzi in the apartment. (2) By the protections of the lease, they could force him to make significant repairs to the apartment. (3) If they didn't negotiate to buy the apartment now, they could make it nearly impossible for Ron's agent to show the apartment when it came on the market. (4) They could bad-mouth the apartment to anyone who did come through. (5) They could report him to the city for negligence or discrimination. (6) At the end of their lease, they could stop paying rent and not move out. It would take at least a year to get them evicted. Two could play at this game, and I had seen all the moves.

To their credit, Neil and Gina wouldn't take the bait, not that this stopped discussions from getting ugly. For a month, Ron rotated between yelling and hanging up on his agent, his attorney, and even me. We politely ignored his artificial deadlines, reminded him of his legal obligations, raised our offer price, and, finally, after making our best offer (which included both firms reducing their commissions, I might add), spent a fraught weekend in suspense. Gina was certain

Ron would not come around and accept the revised terms. I convinced myself he would. And he did.

Again, Neil and Gina could have found another rental or option to buy at any point. New York City is the most liquid real estate market in America, with hundreds upon hundreds of available options at any given time, and nearly 10,000 home sales in most years. But all this wrestling with Ron served a bigger purpose. It was their crisis of faith, what has been called the "dark night of the soul." In the language of the hero's journey, this is the Ordeal—its climax, or as Joseph Campbell puts it, the Apotheosis.

It was also exactly what they needed to take back the power in their lives. I'll explain. For so many years, they had let jobs, salaries, and other people's advice determine their moves—and had spent a decade regretting it. They had lost their direction in the suburbs. Their big leap had been to move back into the city. When things got out of control, though, their thermostat kicked in, and back they went to being victims of circumstance. Ron was only too happy to play the role of victimizer and oppressor to perfection. Neil and Gina had pushed themselves to the breaking point. But they weren't the same people who had given up on Manhattan and stopped chasing their dreams years before. These negotiations allowed their new self-image to catch up to them, and helped them out of this valley of despair. Not only was this the right apartment, but the closing sealed that decision to return to the city with every fiber of their being. We'll return to them later.

🏠 🏠 🏠

These dark nights of the soul, which provide the hardest-won wisdom along your journey, often show up as an unexpected decision to make, after you thought you had already made it. In some cases, you'll be presented with a last-second chance to get out of your purchase. It's a tempting off-ramp, to be sure.

The day before Seth—an analytical, quiet, number-crunching hedge-fund founder—closed on a top-floor Tribeca loft purchase, we noticed during the walk-through (which I'll describe in more detail in the next chapter) that the kitchen looked off—really off. Ravaged is a better word, with gaping spaces where the fridge, oven, and dishwasher had been. It seemed the seller, a French race car driver, had the movers pack up and move out all the appliances! This is commonplace in France and elsewhere in Europe. It also happens to be a violation of real estate sales contracts in New York. Normally cool-minded Seth was in a rage. He called his attorney, who pointed out that, strictly speaking, he could walk away from his purchase without penalty if he wished.

Seth fell right into the trap the universe set. He reopened his spreadsheets and rehashed every analysis he had done. We did another market review together. Had prices dipped one iota since he signed his contract? His well-trained logical side was fighting so zealously against his emotions that he could only vaguely remember he was buying this property well below market value. He completely forgot that these 30-year-old appliances would have gone in the trash the second his extensive renovations began. Had the listing agent and I not negotiated a small discount from the seller, Seth would have thrown his house away too.

Some buyers become so distraught that they invent excuses rather than wait for them. In most markets, good-faith deposits are only a few thousand dollars. In New York City, it's 10% of the purchase price—quite a lot more. Buyers have chosen to permanently abandon massive down payments when they have only temporarily lost their minds. After 20 years in real estate, I have yet to see an ejection made in haste prove out. Clients are, without fail, full of regret later.

🏠 🏠 🏠

Has it ever occurred to you that we might drum up drama so we can save ourselves? A house, too, can provide the platform for such acts of self-created sabotage and subsequent heroism. Much can be learned from them both.

Dan and Rebecca's marriage stood on the edge of breaking apart. They had already separated, sold their apartment, and moved into different rentals before they decided to give themselves a second chance. That included hiring me so they could find a new home free of any past misgivings. The universe would soon mightily test their belief in this plan, however.

Jared represented the seller of the property we were pursuing. In the spirit of transparency, I felt a sit-down was in order to clarify my clients' reconciliation. He was bristlier than I expected. "I wish you had told me this earlier," he mused, clearly irked. With his head tilted and his left eyebrow raised, he said, "Are you sure that he isn't just buying an apartment for his ex-wife and kids?" In any other city, no one would blink an eye about such a transaction. But in New York City, the land of cooperative apartments, the co-op board is king. And every real estate agent, especially listing agents, lives in constant fear that a board will turn down their buyer.

The approval process when buying a cooperative apartment can be arbitrary and even prejudicial. Retirees with more assets than they'll ever need, but who live on a fixed income, see their balance sheet put under serious scrutiny. I've seen successful professional women, especially single mothers, be discriminated against when compared to single men. God forbid you own stock in a company deemed environmentally unfriendly, or have ever supported the wrong politician (since your donations are a matter of public record). You could be blackballed from a building for ever having an untoward press mention.

Don't forget the veterinarian's stamp of approval. Your dog may need to be weighed, interviewed, and brought into the elevator to see how it behaves around other owners' pets.

Jared worried that this co-op might dig deeper into Rebecca's lack of income were they to believe she was in actuality living by herself, or ask for paperwork about their separation and what it instructed Dan to pay her, or worse, reject the sale altogether. It didn't help that Jared was divorced himself. Clearly, he was skeptical that anyone could get back together.

I was concerned too; this two-to-three-month purchase process might end in a rejection, which could have spelled the end for Dan and Rebecca. I felt a responsibility to avert that at all costs. However, each of us had a different strategy for doing so. Jared preferred a head-on approach. I preferred a softer sell. Maybe they had sold their last apartment to test out different neighborhoods? Why not gloss over the almost-divorce completely? In the end, it was my clients' call. And they tortured themselves with letter revisions until the very last moment that we submitted their application for review.

The board took nearly three weeks to respond. It felt like an eternity. Even the most happily married buyers stress out while they wait, like high school seniors dying to get their college admissions results. And Dan and Rebecca were not exactly happily married, or remarried, in this case—not yet, anyway. They filled the space with endless grousing. I had to run a data analysis of 10 years of property prices just to keep Dan from pulling the plug on the contract and walking away from their down payment. Rebecca would call me, apoplectic, just to cry on my shoulder. The uncertainty was killing them.

I am almost embarrassed to say our original concerns all proved unnecessary; the cooperative board didn't ask a single question about their marital status. But then the plot twisted. The board would only approve the buyers *conditionally*. In order to proceed, Dan and Rebecca would need to place *two years'* worth of the apartment's monthly charges into an escrow account. In some ways, this was more insidious. What was the board *not* saying, or saying behind their backs? That they would need to prove the strength of their personal relationship over time? As thoroughly unsatisfying as this was, it also gave the buyers an out. If they chose not to follow the board's escrow directive, the sale would collapse with a board rejection, but they could get their money back.

Why, you might ask, had Dan and Rebecca knowingly put themselves through this? They could have bought a condominium, thereby skirting a co-op's approval madness. But then they would not have answered their bigger question: Are we sure about saving this marriage? They committed to this more punishing path with all its associated headaches. In doing so, they laid down a gauntlet, and found a new source of confidence and empowerment. They learned that they could redefine themselves as people who overcome what sinks most couples. They could be role models for their children, and show that it is never too late to own your mistakes, and make amends.

Swallowing their pride, they agreed to the condition, and the closing took place without a hitch. Our couple stayed hitched, too, taking on a big renovation before they moved in. That their marriage survived gave this typically sad tale a happier ending.

🏠 🏠 🏠

A house can also be a cruel schoolmistress, however, her lessons meted out unfairly. Some buyers must see their nightmares come to pass. That is, only an actual rejection will force them to reckon with whatever personal changes they need to make before they're wholeheartedly ready to move forward. I didn't expect it would happen to my buyers Stan and Franky, because things had started so delightfully.

They had landed a quickly negotiated, off-market deal with a family relocating to Florida. Everything was proceeding smoothly, until I got a text message from my colleague on the other side. "Scott, we need to talk." This is not the phrase you want to see when a contract is out for signature. I soon learned the deal was off.

I have to back up to explain how unexpected this was. For starters, the buyers' children, the sellers' children, and the building board president's children all attended the same private school. Franky also knew the board president's wife, if we assume dinners and coffees together count as knowing one another. If that weren't enough, the husbands were working jointly on a few business deals too. It seemed that fate had already stepped in and blessed the transaction.

I guess fate had other plans. At an end-of-school-year gathering, the sellers told the board president about their quiet off-market sale in progress, and the board president's wife immediately began trashing my clients. "She had disliked your clients for years," my colleague said. "She found them obnoxious and insinuated that they would not be good additions to the building." And then the final nail in the coffin. "Scott, she essentially guaranteed your buyers would be rejected by the board. The sellers don't want to take that gamble."

What was I missing? My clients' heads were spinning and I needed to attend to them. Over the next six months, they grieved in their own way. Stan called me once a week to share his frustration; I'm sure I was one of many on that call list. Franky processed her now-former friend's betrayal in a less-constructive way—by bad-mouthing her. But I knew they were both hurting far more than they ever let on.

It took about a year, but Stan and Franky finally dusted themselves off and picked themselves back up. They had been turned down by one building, albeit informally, and survived. More than that, they had found a different apartment in another cooperative building, and sailed through the approval process.

That was the backdrop when the closing price was posted online for the property they had lost a year earlier. Guess who bought it? No one other than the board president and his wife. The only horrifying surprise was the price—*$100,000 less* than what Stan and Franky had prepared to pay before the deal went south. I have to believe that at that school function, the insiders couldn't admit that they wanted to buy the apartment for themselves. They were just uniquely awful people who couldn't help themselves from going down the primrose path. You could say Stan and Franky had been in the wrong place at the wrong time.

Or you could look at it like Newton's third law: Every action has an equal and opposite reaction. The resistance grows—the setbacks, the drama, the "random" bad news, etc.—precisely *because* of your progress, not in spite of it. Your effort and commitment bring about whatever personal growth is available to you, and necessary for you. What I am sure of is that the homebuying journey doesn't always give you what you want, but it will give you *exactly* what you need. Stan and Franky's new home surely felt that much more wonderful as a result of having survived their travails.

The Perfect Foil

Although ugly and gross and seemingly pointless, this group of gatekeepers—the co-op board—serves a valuable purpose in at least one important respect: It is the perfect foil. If you still can't connect the dots between the hero's journey version of the Ordeal and the homebuyer's version, consider the co-op board as an enemy of sorts. I have watched couples prepare for their co-op interview like they were defending a doctoral dissertation. I have had families who were too proud to share their bank statements, until they worked out that they might lose their down payment if they didn't. Buyers have broken down in a puddle while gathering financial documents. You must show extraordinary vulnerability to stare down a board's irrationality, elitism, or worse. If you are willing to court this kind of disaster, even reluctantly, you must be sure that this is a property you want, consequences be damned.

The more common enemy, in New York City or anywhere, however, is your lender. Applying for a mortgage will be just as painful as seeking a green light from a cooperative building. Just like a cooperative, you are submitting for someone's approval. Borrowing for the biggest purchase of your life may be the ultimate emotional hot button.

It gets underway with what has been called the "heart attack package," a thick set of printed documents that arrive in your mailbox. One of these forms will show you your projected monthly commitments for the next 30 years, among many other frightening disclosures. You'll be pulled out of the excitement of your purchase, and plopped onto a psychological minefield. It's almost certain to blow you up. Worried about your finances? Here is a list of every closing cost imaginable, many of which you're not likely to be responsible to cover. Feeling successful? Here's where you'll suddenly feel that you're not strong enough financially or good enough personally. Before you know it, you're neck-deep in paperwork, busy trying to please a faceless, nameless panel of loan underwriters in some dated office park in Tennessee, or California, or South Dakota. They might as well be undertakers since you'll feel like death when you're done. You will drive yourself batty trying to satisfy them because you are rightly scared that, at a whim, they can take away your house.

A bank could also make you feel like your *home* isn't enough. Appraisers' priorities are often in direct opposition to yours. You just won a bidding war, and they'll point out five sales near your new home that sold for less. Their low valuation could have financial implications (which I'll discuss in the next chapter). But emotionally, it can also make you feel like you've made a massive mistake.

As I write this, I just completed buying a second home, which included getting a mortgage. I can't recall ever feeling so completely beaten down by a bureaucracy and its ever-changing, incoherent rules. I also experienced acute déjà vu on every call with the mortgage broker. It conjured up the same out-of-control swirl I felt after my mother and father split. The way that mortgage application was going, I grew ever fearful. What if the bank rejected me? And rejection is part of my every working day! I was on the edge of falling apart. I shudder to think how any first-time buyer might react. You will deserve a medal of some kind after enduring either a co-op purchase or a mortgage application process. All real estate agents should have to go through the lending horror show every few years, just to be reminded of its brutality.

Even if you don't need a mortgage, you'll find yourself begging for someone's approval. A housing market with no inventory by itself can be just as competitive and cutthroat. Ask anyone who has written a groveling letter to a seller, its contents summarized like this: "Please accept my over-asking-price offer!" Thinking of renovating, putting an addition on a home, or even removing a tree? Most properties are subject to ordinances, zoning laws, height restrictions, historic designations, land use reviews, and so on. Engaging with community boards, city councils, and homeowners' associations—on their turf—might be the most Herculean test of all. No one can predict the results of these skirmishes. The prospects of victory are tenuous at best, and the defeats more devastating. Put differently, if you want the Real Estate Gods to laugh, just show them your blueprints.

As Is

The universe taketh away, but sometimes it giveth back. What would you do with a second chance to buy your dream house? Picture this: Your deal has died and then, a few weeks or months later, it miraculously comes back to life.

Erin and Chris started looking for their new home together only a few weeks before their wedding. We found a gorgeous condominium just a few blocks from where they had lived. I wasn't sure whether they were more excited about the apartment or the wedding. But the day before they were to sign contracts, Chris lost his job. They watched their dream house slip away—or so they thought. The seller didn't end up finding a buyer for the unit, and they delisted the property and kept their tenant on instead. When it came back on the market for sale, Chris had a new job, and he and Erin did a gut check. Did they still love it? Perhaps they loved it even more, since they were able to negotiate a price meaningfully lower than they had been willing to pay the year before. Was this a reward for their pain and suffering? Or had they done something else to deserve this karmic payback?

I have lost count of how often my buyers have been the beneficiaries of another buyer's board rejection or mortgage denial. When this happens, either you'll be like Erin and Chris, or you won't be able to get over your broken heart. There's no way to predict your reaction. But there's only one way to make peace with every rejection and heartbreak. It's the same thing that will help you rejoice when things finally go your way—which they will.

You'll need to accept every step of your homebuying journey as it is, and accept your dream house in as-is condition. Reframe your homebuying story. Strip away the superficial excitement or the fantasy of the stress-free transaction. The more profound truth to which you must surrender is that everything that's happened so far has happened for a reason. Every person in your transaction—even the most atrocious offenders—was doing the best that they could. So, no more blaming. No more complaining of the twists and turns. They were inescapable. In fact, yours was the perfect journey to your dream house.

Marcus Aurelius, former Roman emperor and practitioner of Stoicism, would have put it this way: "Whatever happens to you has been waiting to happen since the beginning of time. The twining strands of fate wove both of them together: your own existence and the things that happen to you."

Indeed, the Stoics would love the exercise that I am recommending you do. It is a departure from what I generally have my clients do as part of The Magnetic Method, which is mostly a study in positive thinking. In the right context, however, it is valuable to mentally rehearse awful outcomes. Psychologist Gary Klein called this a "pre-mortem," while others label this work *negative visualization*. The Stoics like Epictetus and Aurelius long ago called it *premeditatio malorum*, or a premeditation of all that could go wrong.

> What's the worst thing that could happen?
> What if this drama is happening to *help* you?

One way to look at this book is as one big *premeditatio malorum*! You'll have no trouble inventing mishaps, just as you'll have ideas of how to respond to them as your best self. Then, no matter what happens, you will have new tools and tactics at your disposal.

Now go one step further. Allow for the possibility that these things wouldn't be happening to you, but *for* you. I assure you that it will not take long to see the greater forces working on your behalf.

For instance, one of my buyers later learned he dodged a serious bullet when he lost a bidding war. That apartment wasn't spared from a building-wide leak that put dozens of its owners into hotels for months. Over the years, other buyers have saved millions of dollars on what would have been bad purchases. You'll want to kiss those sellers for spurning your advances. The houses you lost were not only not meant to be—buying one might have been fatal.

You are more than any one transaction, or any one house. And just as that lesson sinks in, that is when the phone call will come— a week, a month, or a year later. Your agent will tell you that a buyer backed out, and that dream property is yours. For instance, after Neil and Gina's debacle and closing, their neighbor's studio apartment came on the market, just in time to turn their dream purchase into their forever home.

God doesn't just give you what you can handle. He wants to give you something to help you evolve, as your older, smaller way of living gives way to something far more substantial. You are not the same person who began looking for a home not so long ago. Stop pretending that you are.

I hope that you will accept this beautiful idea as true, as it portends a lot of good things to come, like what your life looks like in your new house. However, we still must attend to the closing. As you'll see, both getting to the closing table, and the day itself, isn't exactly a walk in the park.

CHAPTER 8

You Can Go
Home Again

The Closing

"A man travels the world over in search of
what he needs and returns home to find it."
—George Moore

Approaching the Finish Line

If finding a home seems like a grueling race with no end in sight, take comfort. The marathon is nearly complete. You will soon be able to see just how worthwhile your efforts have been. I lean on the metaphor of the marathon because I have had the experience of running more than two dozen of them. The marathon's lessons map easily onto our lives—and, like the hero's journey, onto your real estate search as well. Some are obvious. For instance, chasing the elite runners is just as futile as keeping up with the Joneses. Really, the only person you're competing against is yourself.

The most helpful lessons, however, began appearing about a decade ago, when I was forced to put myself back in the shoes of someone who had never run before. After an uncomfortable training run I had to cut short, an MRI showed substantial wear and tear inside both of my hip sockets. While I was a candidate for a laparoscopic procedure, there was no certainty that I would hit the streets again, much less at long distances. The alternative, though, was worse: slowly increasing discomfort, with a near-guarantee that I'd need hip replacements in the not-too-distant future.

Thus, I took a journey into the unknown, just like you have here. I had to choose a doctor who I felt understood my predicament and whose track record was impeccable. Then I had to overcome my fears of general anesthesia, needles, operating rooms, and hospitals; this was my first-ever surgery.

I soon learned it would be more taxing emotionally than it ever was physically. I had been so tied up in my identity as a runner that the fear of not running again was overwhelming. They say that professional athletes die twice. Even as an amateur, I felt like I was dying too. The post-surgery reality was that I couldn't help much around the house or, worse, teach my daughter to ride a bicycle a few months later. While it was uncomfortable to bend over to put on my shoes, my pride was healing more slowly than my hips. I also put on about 10 pounds, between stress eating, not being able to exercise very much, and increasing my alcohol consumption, which seemed like the only thing I could run to. The voices in my head told me that I should just give up running and give in to middle age. Everything they said and everything I did was making things worse.

Only when the doctor-sanctioned recovery plan began did things start to turn around. Yes, I could only run two minutes at a time, then only add a half-mile to my running each week. But there was light at the end of the tunnel. Supportive friends helped me celebrate little achievements. I found a book that helped me rethink my running form. I hired a running coach who told me to run less, and work out more. The possibility of running a full marathon became real again. And I deployed the principles of The Magnetic Method to my own training.

My patience in the process and my faith in my vision were tested more than they ever had been. Yet, 18 months later, I was one of the 51,388 finishers of the 2016 New York Marathon, one of the proudest moments of my life. I had proof that I could begin again. And I came to understand the primary significance of the finish line: It is there so you can look back and see how far you've come. I still train for marathons, but I hold my identity as a runner more lightly. I'm more interested in how it reminds me that I can do whatever I fully commit to. Like writing this book. And I hope that I've inspired you to believe the same is possible for you.

Finding a home is among life's most meaningful accomplishments. Think of your real estate journey. It, too, was just one step after another. You sought out inspiration to get started. You kissed a bunch of frogs and spent way too long addressing everything you didn't like about them. Then you waded through your mental hang-ups and their tempting suggestions of self-sabotage. After your attempts to control everything, you even let go of what you previously thought would make you happy in your new home. You took your life to the studs, as it were. You allowed the universe, in its uniquely frustrating way, to present you with a house with which you were finally ready to fall madly in love.

Despite all of the obstacles, you've gotten here. You will cross that finish line, too, just beyond one more curve in the road: the closing. The last mile is bumpier than you'd expect. It's a sprint that will leave you gasping for air.

The Mad Dash

The days before the closing are always a scramble to sort out details. No matter how many real estate professionals you have working for you, they can't shield you from last-second, maddening paperwork reviews and requests from the lender, the title closer, or your attorney. If you're a planner, plan for this: You won't know the final numbers until very late in the game. That rough draft of your closing costs you received when you first applied for financing are only now reconciled in a closing statement with credits, debits, and lots of line items. What could be more hair-raising than your attorney or lender ominously telling you to bring your checkbook to the closing, just in case there are any discrepancies in the accounting?

Well, I'll tell you. Almost without fail, someone with your name has committed a crime in your state. What fun! A lender will ask you to sign an affidavit that it wasn't you. A title report might list all sorts of discouraging oddities: open construction permits, contractor liens that your sellers didn't know about, or other items that can "cloud" the title. An old friend's title report of his home near Philadelphia revealed that a five-square-foot corner of his backyard was owned by the railroad authority. His bank hadn't caught this detail when he bought, but his buyers couldn't close for months.

The glass-half-full take would emphasize that about three-quarters of closings go off as planned. But you should also know that more than 20% of closings are delayed and roughly 5% of pending offers fall through. As we saw, you could suddenly lose your job. A seller could have a problem with the timing of their own purchase, or could go into cardiac arrest two days before closing, a situation my buyer contended with a few years ago (the deal eventually closed). Occasionally, a seller gets cold feet and tries to kill the sale altogether. Then it will be you with heart problems.

Let's say you applied for a new credit card at your favorite big-box store a week before your closing. That could blow your credit score. Or you could change jobs between contract and closing. Don't do these things! The federal guidelines or the bank's underwriting parameters could also change mid-transaction and reduce the size of your mortgage. More commonly, a low bank appraisal might jeopardize what your bank is willing to lend you—and wreak unforeseen havoc.

In the best of times it still takes a small village to get to the closing table. Who attends? You, your agent and the seller's agent, the sellers or their representative, the lender officer, the title company, and also, depending on where you live, two real estate attorneys. In New York City, add to this all the cooperative's staff. Coordinating all these people is an exercise in herding cats. You aren't the shepherd (it's usually an attorney, title closer, or agent), but all it takes is one sick child, a death in the family, or a holiday to throw things off. Meanwhile, you have scheduled your movers or have not renewed your lease. You could be staring down the barrel of expensive temporary housing, or a week with your in-laws.

Intellectually, you know it wouldn't be helpful if your team got caught up in the whirlwind, but it's also upsetting that they aren't as discombobulated as you are. The agents involved seem like they're not moving quickly enough. I think of the one time in the last few decades that I played racquetball. It was against a much older guy, a scraggly, hunched-over attorney who looked like he hadn't exercised much in years. Apparently, that didn't keep him from being a gifted player. He seemed not to move more than a step here and there, as I ran in every direction to smack the little blue rubber ball. I was red in the face and out of breath, and he put out no more energy than if he had been sipping a teacup with his pinky up. It made me furious. He was just more experienced at playing the game than I was.

The Walk-Through

What might finally make your excited and tired legs buckle beneath you, though, is the pre-closing property tour, known as a walk-through. It's usually your last chance to visit your new home, scheduled the day before the closing, and double-check that nothing has changed since you signed the contracts, or to confirm that the seller followed through on promises to repair certain items. It's as if someone said, "What would guarantee that buyers lose all their joy and excitement? I know! Let's have them look for anything that's wrong."

The walk-through thrusts you back into Opposite Mode from chapter 4, where you could only point out the negatives in a house. There's one difference. *This is the home you're buying!* The situation is combustible, and the tiniest thing will set off the explosion. You'll notice a nick in a window screen. A stain on the floor previously hidden underneath a rug. A wall damaged during the move-out. A nonfunctioning outlet. A dripping faucet. A dust bunny where a couch used to be. Maybe even, God forbid, a dead cockroach or mouse droppings. Many of these "issues" were there before, but you were too excited to catch them. Others were avoidable if the seller or their agent owned a broom, or some common sense. In either case, though, the only reason they become a big deal is that the house is effectively under a microscope.

I have provided a comprehensive *Pursuit of Home* Walk-Through Checklist in the appendix, also available online.† Its room-by-room recommendations may help you keep your wits about you. But with or without it in your hand, you're likely to go berserk. The conversations and questions ensue during and after the walk-through between you and your agent, your attorney, and your friends and family. *Can you believe this? What a jerk! Did they do this on purpose? Should we delay the closing? What should we do?* I would be more astounded if you didn't lose your temper at least once. One buyer told me he felt like a dog with fleas for the two weeks leading up to the closing, waking up itchy in the middle of the night. Most agents will not confess that they feel like they often lose control of their buyers right before the closing. You might feel like your tail is wagging both you and your agent.

> Bring the printed-out walk-through checklist, plug-in phone charger, and phone with you to the walk-through. Take clear notes and document what you see with video and photos.

It's worth mentioning the other side of the transaction at this point. Sellers aren't likely to engage with your overreactions. They already have plenty of worries of their own. They've been living in this house for years and managing their own emotions about leaving. They might be getting divorced or moving reluctantly into assisted living. They might be losing money on the sale and angry at everyone but themselves about it, or, conversely, have a boatload of taxes to pay. The sellers could be the exhausted executors of their deceased parents' estate, and just finished cleaning everything out for you. Don't

---

† Take a look at www.pursueyourhome.com/walkthrough.

forget that you might have waltzed into someone else's stress. The walk-through has just made it worse.

This isn't to let anyone off the hook. Some sellers are so oblivious they cancel their utilities so you can't check the power during your walk-through. Others will knowingly try to get away without honoring their commitments. The seller's agent might be unscrupulous too. You, your agent, and your attorney should hold them accountable. But these fights are unappetizing precisely because everyone is making mountains out of molehills instead of talking about the real stuff that's too scary, sad, or exciting to mention. The walk-through is a poor stand-in for all of it.

🏠 🏠 🏠

Now let's raise the stakes to a point that will seem ludicrous, but is not out of the ordinary at all, since nearly one in five homebuyers in 2022 bought a newly constructed home. There is a roughly 20% chance you'll have not one, but two walk-throughs. The first one, a few days or a few weeks before the closing, packs an extra punch, because you're expected to document all of the home's construction defects or cosmetic imperfections. The list you generate is the basis for what's known colloquially as a *punch list*. It's the working document that outlines anything that needs to be repaired before closing. You might wonder how a normal person would be expected to even understand what construction defects are. You might also assume that your real estate agent, who probably isn't a contractor, would recommend you hire an inspector to come in and assist in this punch list walk-through. You would be wrong. I know, it's dismaying. In most states, real estate agents guide you through this process, walking through the house with a representative for the home builder. But some builders won't allow them to attend either!

Emotionally speaking, one walk-through would be enough to knock you flat. But you've already waited eons for the house to be completed and are only just seeing the final product. How overwhelming would this be? Imagine the anticipation, the adrenaline, plus the trepidation and the pressure. You're supposed to just slap on a hard hat and calmly tour your new space with a clipboard in your hand? With every scratch, the letdown is magnified. You expected perfection. You'll get disappointment.

Think about this through the eyes of the different Buyer Personalities we met in chapter 3. How will they each engage with the punch list? The Homebody might see the punch list as an affront to their children's safety. The Designer might be so turned off to the house because the quality of construction and the little details are so important to their eye. The Good Neighbor is incredibly conflicted. This is a pretty serious confrontation, both with their agent and the seller—especially if there are a lot of dents, dings, or blemishes. This will put a serious strain on these relationships. The House Manager will defer to the agent to make sure everything looks as it should. And do I even need to tell you how the Meter Reader will react? The laundry list of faults will be longer than your arm.

Early in my career, I strolled blindly into a nearly catastrophic punch list walk-through. My buyer, Teddy, had only ever seen the gorgeous showroom of the SoHo building that he was buying six months earlier. Developers will often prohibit building visits during construction. They'll say it's for safety reasons. But it is primarily because of what happened two weeks before this closing, when we toured the apartment for the initial walk-through. His fantasy was pierced by the stark reality of what tradespeople invariably leave behind. There were broken floor tiles, scuff marks on the baseboards, poorly installed light switches and other construction debris. One worker had even drawn some lewd graffiti in the outside hallway that was yet to be painted, a reminder that this wasn't built by fairies, but by flesh-and-blood people who were also eating lunch at some point on the floor of his living room.

It was never going to be about the two-page punch list we created. Those items would be repaired, even if in this case it took some arm twisting to get the builder to do what the contract required. It was largely about managing Teddy's expectations properly beforehand. I would describe his Buyer Personality as that of a Designer. For him, walking into that apartment was like reentering the atmosphere from space. And he did not have the right front shield to protect his ship from the heat. I blame myself to a large degree. I could have helped him avoid most of the panic attacks from that day.

Amos and Corinne had to wait even longer for their downtown penthouse apartment to be completed. As the building grew taller, we further discussed their concerns: *Has the real estate market shifted since we signed contracts? How are the other units selling? Is the quality of the finishes as good as we saw in the sales office? Is the developer strong enough financially to see this through? Are we buying in a nice enough building? Is the reputation of the building developing as beautifully as its facade?* What they weren't saying: As thrilling as this was, as much as they loved the space, it was uncomfortable as hell to wait.

By that point in my career, I also anticipated what was coming. When the wait is over, the punch list is the only means through which most buyers let this flood of long-awaited emotions come out. Not the most constructive method. In this case, Amos was a House Manager and Corinne was a Homebody. She went nuclear after our punch list walk-through for reasons of safety. To assuage her, Amos hired consultants to build their case. They hired construction experts. They threatened lawsuits over defects. They insinuated that they would go to the press. They asked to visit other new buildings represented by the same sales team so the developer would know about it. And they eloquently pointed out that losing the penthouse buyer would be potentially ruinous to the builder's credibility and bottom line.

Getting to the closing took an extra four months, and we estimated about $200,000 of the developer's time and materials. Did Amos and Corinne need thousand-dollar-an-hour attorneys to negotiate on their behalf? Probably not. Did they have to play hardball to get their way? Yes, but only because they instigated a battle that required it. It wasn't about the time, nor the money, nor perfection, nor control. They just needed to be satisfied they had done everything possible to have the space they had been dreaming of for so long. They needed those extra skirmishes to somehow feel they had earned it, so Corinne could feel her family would be both safe and happy, and so Amos could feel that he had the investment and value in place, and the vision in his mind fully executed upon.

Regardless of your own Buyer Personality, no one comes out of a walk-through unscathed. The details and defects are almost immaterial. It's just nearly impossible to avoid using this venue to release your buildup of emotions. If you need any further proof that you will need a patient team to help get you across the finish line, this is it.

🏠 🏠 🏠

The walk-through brings together your heightened jumble of emotions and reality. Will you break down in a puddle of tears? Perhaps not if you're a House Manager, but you probably will if you're a Homebody. And nearly everyone tries to put a price tag on their hurt feelings. In the jargon of real estate, these are called closing credits. The questions head in this direction: *How much should the seller give us? How much should we ask for? How are they going to respond?* With a larger repair, you'll want to guarantee the seller fixes it for you, especially if you are feeling the pressure of a deadline. You may have to ask the seller to put money into escrow, held by your attorney, until the problem is resolved.

The bigger questions are these: What are you looking for from this negotiation? And what will you get in the end? You may squeeze $500 or $5,000 from a seller, but I promise you it will never feel like enough. You won't feel true satisfaction, nor real vengeance. Nothing good will come from these petty arguments. Again, it's the end of a long, long journey. And like an argument you manufacture when you must say goodbye to someone you love after a wonderful vacation, it's easier to leave angry than sad.

You might be buying a tear-down or planning a massive renovation. That could immunize you against these squabbles. Otherwise, there's almost no way to avoid them. The best advice I have for coming out whole on the other side? Follow what many philosophers and religious traditions have called the Silver Rule. It's not the Golden Rule, where you do unto others as you would have them do unto you. It's the inverse. Don't do anything you wouldn't want done to you. Simply put, don't be a jerk, since you don't want the seller to be a jerk to you.

I would recommend you take the high road, even if the seller chooses not to reciprocate. This isn't a court case in which you're angling for damages. Pretend this seller is going to be your neighbor, that you're going to run into them in the grocery store, or at social gatherings, or in your house of worship. Not plausible enough? What if your local paper were going to write about your purchase on the front page? At the risk of sounding trite, you will feel better knowing that you've created the possibility that you can look your seller in the eye and shake hands after the closing is over.

There may not be a graceful exit to the high road, of course. In that case, try not to get your hands dirty. Let your professionals advocate for you and stay out of it as much as you can. Before you protest, know this: You're not being a pushover. You're giving yourself some much-needed love and caring, after what has been an arduous journey. In doing so, you shift all your energy away from your lesser angels, and the seller's. Best of all, the negotiations will go much better. And having done all you could, I bet you'll sleep better at night, in your bed in your new home.

The Finish Line

When this commotion subsides, what do you get? Eerie silence. You've been waiting for this day! The closing is here. And it's the opposite of what you expect. Dig around online for closing table advice. What will you find? "Bring your favorite pen and a checkbook." No guide mentions that the actual closing isn't a ceremony. It's an anticlimax.

The herded cats shuffle in, a motley crew in various states of dress. Really, it's almost in reverse order of who will have the most money at the end. The staff and attorneys are in business suits, the agents are in business casual, and the seller is almost always wearing athleisure. Where do you fit in? Somewhere in the middle. Think about it. By the time you get here, you're exhausted. Like a marathon, you just want to stop running, not put on a fancy outfit.

That doesn't stop everyone else from treating the closing like a cocktail party, even if they have nothing to offer but the most awkward banter. The agents are trying to keep it light, but beneath their cheer, they are either seething at the other agent in the room, or quietly praying that neither you nor the seller says something to reopen negotiations or leave things on a sour note. They'll distract you with stilted softball questions about your kids and your upcoming vacations. You're right to sense that the sellers—and let's face it, everyone else—are just waiting to take their checks and leave.

Ten states don't even require buyers and sellers to be in the same place for the closing. You'll either sign at your attorney's sterile conference room, or sign at home, and overnight papers to them. No pleasantries and no discernible denouement. Not even the exchange of keys, which may have to wait a day for bank funding to clear. Without question, it's the weirdest part of buying a home. It would make for awful television.

Things only get interesting if they don't go to plan. I once had a buyer show up to a townhouse closing $600,000 short. He ultimately negotiated a personal loan from the already-wealthy seller that enabled him to wrap up the deal. That closing took eight hours. At least I had a heads-up. My buyer had called me the night before and asked me to lend him the money, which I didn't exactly have sitting around. Other agents might have wanted to watch that slow-motion train wreck. I stayed away. I've never liked horror movies.

Still in the cards may be last-minute, leftover negotiations over broken appliances or other items come upon during the walk-through. Some buyer agents treat them as shakedowns, attempting to look like a hero in your eyes by squeezing a few more dollars from a seller. Those interactions can get ugly in a hurry. Other transactions have been so nasty from start to finish that buyers and sellers—or even agents who can't stand each other—must be seated in separate rooms, with papers shuttling back and forth between them. But sometimes there is comic relief. Once, a lender's representative thought she showed up with the funding for the buyer's loan, only to notice that a $350,000 bank check had gone missing somewhere between her office and the location for the closing. I had never seen someone go from perfectly dry to soaking wet in a business suit before, like she had dived into an invisible swimming pool.

Does this make you want to bypass the closing table? If you expected a jamboree with a marching band, you will be let down. In more than 20 years, I have seen only one buyer burst into tears at the closing table. No one else had the energy left to express that level of jubilation, or even relief. I hope that yours will be the happy exception. But don't count on it.

The Post-Closing Possession

However the closing gets done, you'll eventually have the keys in your hands. You've earned your house—the badge of the hero's journey called the Reward. Put the key in the lock. Open the door. If you are still holding your breath from the closing, exhale, take off your battle armor, and have a look around. It's yours. Can you let yourself soak it all in? Say it with me: *It's good to be home.* Hold on to that sentiment for as long as you can. Because just as quickly, a new stage sets in: the Road Back. It will likely throw you a curveball or two. You could forget why you chose to do this.

More than a decade ago, my wife, my kids, and I were scheduled to leave New York and fly to Savannah, Georgia, to join my side of the family for Thanksgiving. But as often happens with preschool children, our younger daughter got an ear infection the day before the trip. So she and my wife stayed home instead.

By 9 PM that Wednesday evening, my older daughter had settled into her cot for bedtime. I was staring at the outline of a fake plant in the corner of a dark hotel room. I could not turn on a light or a television while she slept—not if I wanted her to stay asleep, anyway. And with an only slightly milder version of the cold that sidelined my daughter, I felt pretty lousy myself. I should have been the one to stay back with her, but the pull of obligation had been too strong.

I went into the bathroom to check in with my wife by phone and quietly say good night. As I walked in, I looked in the mirror. Maybe it was the silence, where all I heard was my daughter's breathing. Maybe it was the cold medicine I had taken. Maybe it was my fear of missing out, since everyone else was together downstairs at the bar.

Or it was just me hitting bottom. I was overwhelmed with a profound loneliness and a sadness deeper than I had ever remembered feeling. Along with it came a sudden awareness. *I don't want to be here anymore. I just want to be home.*

I flashed back to being eight years old, right after my parents separated, shuttling between the only house I had ever known and my father's recently rented one-bedroom apartment. I again felt the suffocating, looming dread of those evenings when my brother and I would squeeze our clothes into a green faux-leather suitcase and stuff our toys into a little canvas zip-up bag. I could count on either parent to be punctual. But my life was otherwise unsettled, even as the multi-day back and forth became a once-a-week transition. Then I thought of the half a decade in my 20s, when I slept in much scabbier hotel rooms than the one I was currently in, while on tour after tour with my band. I loved meeting all of those people and performing for them. But through all that traveling, I had also re-created the most trying element of my childhood.

All I had ever wanted was somewhere I didn't have to leave as soon as I had arrived. And I already had one: my home. *Why was I still traveling for Thanksgiving when I could be there now? I could celebrate this holiday not in a hotel, but in my dining room. You know what? I get to celebrate anytime I want.* The full weight of this recognition hit me. Home was a refuge, a place to recharge, learn, and celebrate. A repatterning of the misguided belief that love can't last. A physical commitment to healing the broken home of my childhood.

It was also a space to gather everyone and help them feel welcome, where I could show up as the best, most authentic, most openhearted version of myself, where I could put my gratitude on display, and share in my blessings. Admitting what home was for me changed how I engaged with the world. It transformed my business into what it is today.

I believe that the work real estate agents do, manifesting dreams into form, is somehow consecrated. Home is the essence of who we are. It is baked into the language of real estate. We get *renovation* from the Latin roots *re-*, "again," and *novare*, "to make new"; the word we use in English was pulled from the medieval church, where it referred to the "spiritual rebirth wrought by the Holy Spirit." Heady stuff.

The word *home* derives from the Latin word *hominem*, or "human." This same connection appears in all Romance languages: *hombre* in Spanish, *homme* in French, and *uomo* in Italian. We have always been intertwined with our homes. You could say a house cannot become a home without a person, and a person can't live fully without a home. You and your home are like yin and yang, sacred opposites, magnetized to one another.

Your mortgage has serious meaning, too, combining the Old French for "death" (*mort*) and "pledge" (*gage*). Even more profound is its Modern Hebrew counterpart, *mashkanta*. Instead of using the word *arabh* from the Bible, *mashkanta* derives from the biblical Tabernacle, *mishkan*, the dwelling place of God on Earth. So it's no longer just a loan. It's how you turn your home into *your* tabernacle. Doesn't their interpretation make perfect sense, though? You have gone through hell, through high water, confronted your fears, and entered a completely different world of acceptance. This is the power that the home search has had in your life. And how can you say you were ever really alone in this journey? Haven't you, in effect, created your own holy place in which the universe's presence can be felt?

What does home mean to you? If you are not sure yet, you now have a place, the best place, in which to search for the answer. I am fortunate to get to ask this question of my clients. Their responses go to the heart of what animates us, and to what gives us hope, courage, spirit, and purpose. So will yours. Home is a story, a person, an idea, a feeling, or some combination of them all. Every songwriter tries to put lyrics around it. Your unique answer is the most valuable guide you possess. It's what got you here.

This is the perfect moment to explore yourself. To do that, I offer you an exercise called the Seven Levels Deep Exercise.† I stumbled upon it during a Tony Robbins and Dean Graziosi self-help program. I saw how it could sneak into anyone's heart like a ninja, and uncover what drives them to achieve any major life goal. We'll apply it to finding your dream home. It starts with this question: *Why is finding a new home important to you?* Pause to jot down your answer. From there, fill in the next level, asking why that reason is important to you. Just keep going and pausing until you've gone seven levels deep.

For example, finding your dream home may be important because you want to have a place where you feel happy and comfortable. Feeling happy and comfortable in your home is important because it creates a space where you can relax and recharge after a long day. Having a space where you can relax and recharge is important because it helps you maintain your mental and physical well-being. Maintaining your mental and physical well-being is important because you want to be more present and productive in your daily life. Being more present and productive in your daily life is important because it enables you to achieve your goals and spend quality time with loved ones. Achieving your goals and spending quality time with loved ones is important because it gives your life purpose and strengthens your relationships with the people you care most about. And having purpose and strong relationships is important because it makes you feel fulfilled, satisfied, and connected, which is ultimately what you want from life—and what you've always dreamed of.

I always end up crying when I do this exercise.

---

† Find the Seven Levels Deep Exercise at www.pursueyourhome.com/7levels deep.

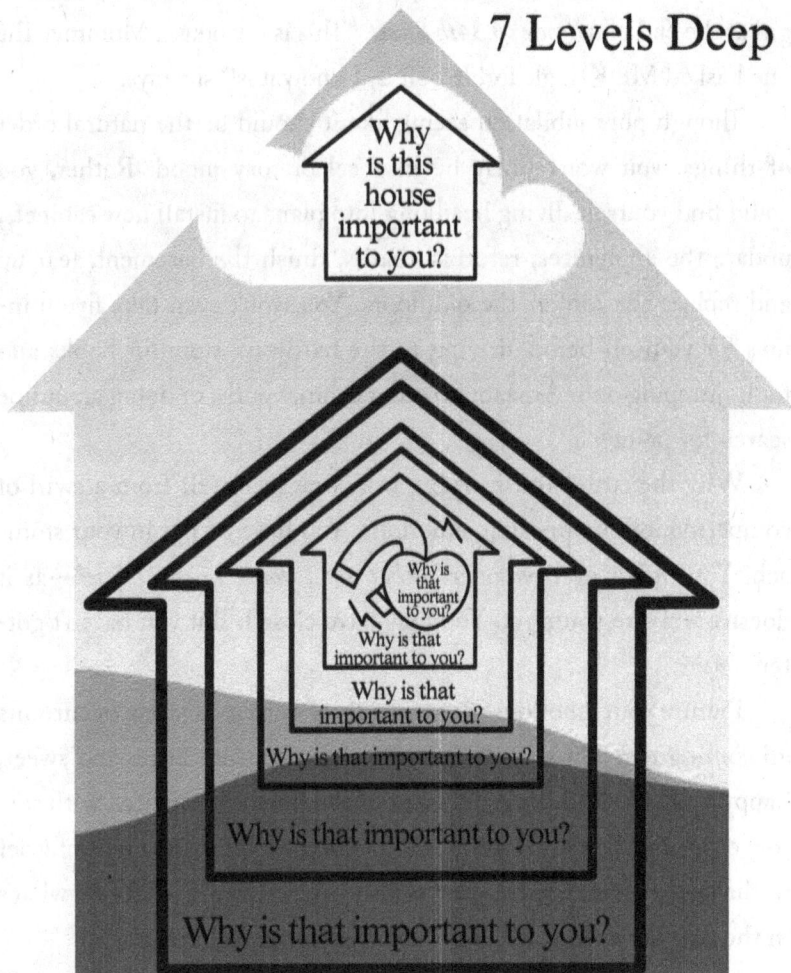

7 Levels Deep

Why is this house important to you?

Why is that important to you?

Why is that important to you?

Why is that important to you?

Why is that important to you?

Why is that important to you?

Why is that important to you?

The Reveal

Reality diverges from television one last time, after the closing. I'm thinking of so many episode finales, when the buyers get to see the finished product. Cue the sweeping music and the camera pull-back. The curtain is lifted to reveal the house, or the front door swings open. It's called *the reveal*. It's supposed to be a *revelation*. This has really happened!

You've made it to the mountaintop. You should feel like Susie, the little girl at the end of *Miracle on 34th Street*. "This is my house, Mommy! The one I asked Mr. Kringle for! It is, it is, I know it is!" she says.

Though pure jubilation seems like it should be the natural order of things, you won't likely be in a celebratory mood. Rather, you could find yourself diving headlong into plans to install new cabinets, update the appliances, refurbish baths, finish the basement, tear up and replace the roof or the old floors. You won't even take five minutes for yourself before driving to the hardware store for hooks and tools, jumping onto Amazon to order cabinet pulls, or doing an online search for painters.

Why the rush? You're trying to distract yourself from a swirl of competing, often opposing, emotions. You have a knot in your stomach. You might even wonder: *What am I doing in this house?*—as it doesn't feel like yours yet. You may have closed. But you haven't gotten *closure*.

Picture your emotions as the mouth of a river, its layers of currents all coming together as it dumps into the ocean. It's bitter and sweet, happy and sad. And the excitement of the future gets paired with sorrow of losing the past. I know we touched on the four stages of grief in the last chapter. Oddly, grief is also the best way to describe what's in the way between you and celebrating your new home.

My close friend and his wife had years to imagine how he would feel when his father finally succumbed to the damaging effects of Alzheimer's. They expected to feel relief and when he passed away recently, they quickly forgot the grumpy shell of a man his father had become. However, still underneath was the overwhelming grief of loss for who he had been before the illness. It's strange but true to say that closing on a house is like losing a loved one. Except that loved one is you. You've stepped off the Road Back, and you're experiencing what Joseph Campbell would call the Resurrection stage of the hero's

journey. Once you recover from the craziness of the homebuying journey itself, you're left to adjust to the fact that you are not the same
person you were before.

♠ ♠ ♠

How long will it take to start feeling like your new self? When will
you be able to fully inhabit the seven-levels-deep version of yourself
who knows what is most important? I'd avoid attempting a prediction
on that one. But if you want to give yourself a nudge in the right
direction, I have two recommendations. Number one, put any urges
to renovate or decorate into this context: as a wonderful way to make
a home feel more like yours. Ground your decision-making in *why
home is important to you*. You are likely to take different, more impact-
ful actions that both benefit the space you can see and enhance *you*
simultaneously. Metaphorically speaking, the second story you add
onto your house should somehow create a new story in your life too.
Nineteenth-century social reformer Charles Henry Parkhurst once
said that "home is heaven for beginners." Make sure you strive to
make that true. Otherwise, you're selling yourself short.

Second, ink in a date on the calendar for a party in your house
before you have even closed. It will give you something to look forward to, through the lender insanity, walk-through craziness, closing table disappointments, and mixed emotions. Don't worry if you
won't have enough furniture. That only gives you reason to invite more
people. Don't wait for things to be just right. You've already got the
perfect space. Plan a real celebration right away. And get ready to fill
your home with the joy it—and you—deserve. This is how you come
home again. Your Eden isn't right around the corner. It's here already.

But your home is ready for more than a party. There is in fact a much
bigger payoff. We'll look at what's in store for you in the next chapter.

CHAPTER 9

The Launch Pad

How Homes Show
Their Appreciation

"Home is where your story begins."
—Annie Danielson

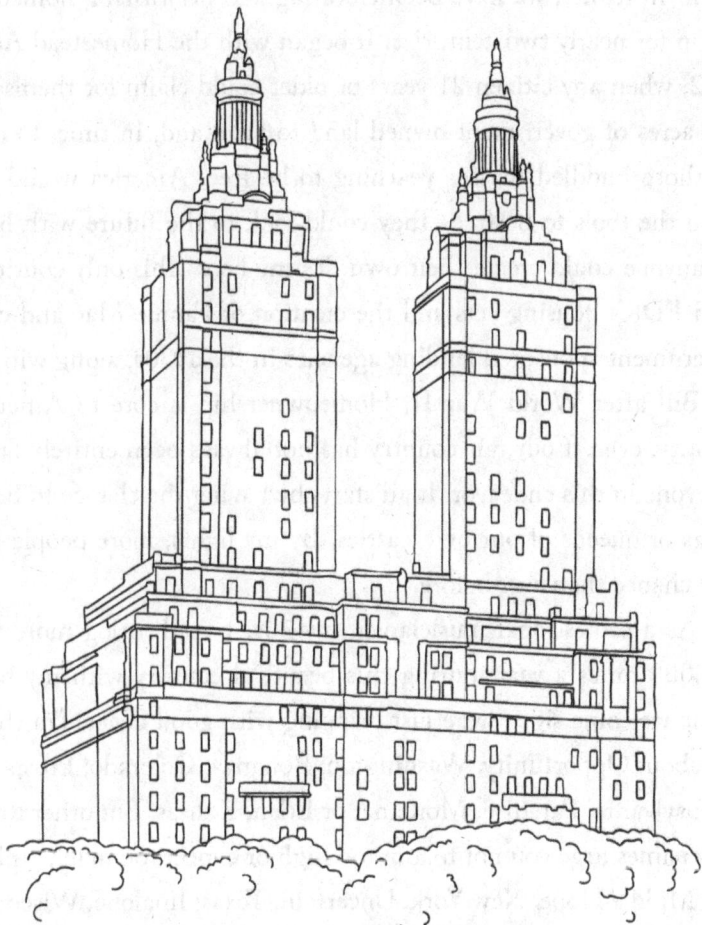

Bringing It All Back Home

I have framed the homebuying journey as a hero's journey, but the search for a dream home in the United States is much more than a myth. In reality, we have been elevating and prioritizing homeownership for nearly two centuries. It began with the Homestead Act of 1862, when any citizen 21 years or older could claim for themselves 160 acres of government-owned land to farm and, in time, to own. To those huddled masses yearning to be free, America would give them the tools to be free. They could look to the future with hope, for anyone could create their own destiny here. This only continued with FDR's housing acts and the creation of Fannie Mae and other government-sponsored lending agencies in the 1930s, along with the GI Bill after World War II. Homeownership is core to American identity, even if our fair country has not always been entirely fair to everyone in this endeavor. It all starts by having the chance to be the kings or queens of our own castles. By my lights, more people have that chance than ever before.

As a professional musician in my 20s, I used to log more than 100,000 miles a year touring this beautiful country with my band. Some welcome signs were just dripping with good cheer. I'm thinking about Opportunity, Washington; Bonanza, Colorado; Prosperity, Pennsylvania; Paradise, Montana; or Eden, Kansas. But other towns' very names urge you not to aim too high or expect too much—places like Middle Hope, New York; Uncertain, Texas; Imalone, Wisconsin; Lost City, West Virginia; Idiotville, Oregon; or even Hell, Michigan.

Whatever your starting point, don't downplay what you have overcome to get here. You found the motivation to counteract the pull of staying in place. You surrounded yourself with professionals who kept you on track, yes, but it was you who fought the uphill battle of conquering your fears, hearing those internal voices who told you this goal wasn't possible—and powering through their efforts to derail you. More than that, you began to believe in your vision, and in doing so, brought your dream home into material form. And yet even when things continued to look bleak, when lenders, sellers, other difficult people, or other grueling stumbling blocks presented themselves, you never accepted defeat. You have acquired a tangible marker of your progress, and no one can ever take that inner progress away from you. You have arrived at the Return stage of the hero's journey. You have new powers to offer to yourself, your family, your community, and beyond.

You also have a lot to be proud of. So celebrating your new home is not just to show it off to your friends. It is an essential pause in the journey you took to get here. I will borrow an exercise from the business world that is well suited to ring in this moment: the exit interview. What was created to give companies helpful feedback from employees on their way out—voluntarily or not—offers a holistic way for you to think about your homebuying experience. I present the Homeowner Exit Interview. Don't just pinpoint what you've learned, either. Identify the true mileposts of your journey, before you forget them. That is, what it really looked like—and not just the highlights. Think of it as gathering the "outtakes" of the realest real estate reality show ever.

> Gather the real lessons from your homebuying journey before you forget them. How can you best share them with family and friends?

The Homeowner Exit Interview

This includes many of the questions that I have used to interview homebuyers before I have them on my podcast, *The Pursuit of Home*. The best way to describe the podcast is as follows: real people buying real estate. Take a few minutes to put your newfound wisdom into your own words, enabling you to share those helpful nuggets with your friends and family.

Getting Off the Couch

- When did you grasp that it was time to move? What was the driving force?
- How long did it take between when you knew you were ready for a new home and when you started your search? What excuses did you make before you did?
- What finally inspired you to get off the couch or computer and into actual homes?

Starting the House Hunt

- What's your Homebuyer Personality? What about your significant other? How did knowing your tendencies help you in your search? How did it help you hire an agent?
- How did you start? Did you hire an agent right away? Or did you look on your own beforehand? And if you worked with someone, how did you find them? Did you interview multiple people? What was the deciding factor in choosing that one agent in the end?
- Was this your first purchase? If not, what helpful things did you bring from prior experience(s)? On the other hand, what wasn't helpful at all?
- Who led the buying process? You? Your significant other? Your agent?
- What did preparation look like before you started seeing houses? How clear was your vision of your new home? Did you start by creating a

checklist, like what we offered in the Buyer Intake Questionnaire? Or did you just dive right in?

In the Trenches

- How often was your agent your coach? How often your real estate advisor? Which did you need more, their real estate wisdom or their understanding of you and your needs?
- Did you ever fire an agent and hire someone new? Did you fire more than one agent? What was the issue? Was it the same issue over and over? Dare I ask: Was the issue inside you, when it came down to it?
- What did your agent do well during the property search? What about negotiations? What didn't you like about your agent during the property search?
- What was the ugliest property you saw in your search? Where did you disagree with your partner? How long did it take to start agreeing, or at least coming to a compromise? Did you lose out on a property that felt like "the one that got away"? Did that happen multiple times? How long did you spend in Opposite Mode?
- What else went wrong in your purchase process? Who were your houseguests that paid a visit during the search? Where did they steer you wrong? Are you able to laugh about it yet?

When You Found the One

- How long did it take to find your home? And who found it—you or your agent?
- How well did your early vision of your home and the home you bought match up? How much free will did you think you had in your decision? How much did thinking factor in? Or be honest: Was it more intuition?
- What "miracles" took place during your search? Did you use Home Delivery to let your home come to you?
- How important was the price of the home you ultimately bought? Did you spend more than you expected? By how much?

- Did you second-guess your home once you found it?
- Who created more drama in the transaction—you or your significant other, the seller, or the agents involved? Did you have any "dark nights of the soul" when your worst fears came true?

After the Closing

- What were the greatest things to overcome in this transition?
- What did you learn about yourself in the buying process?
- Was there anything that you gave up on that you regret? Any other regrets with your purchase?
- What could your agent have done to make the experience better? What would you have done differently?
- What one piece of wisdom would you share with first-time homebuyers to help them?

🏠 🏠 🏠

There's more to that last question than just encouraging you to be helpful. Even as most homeowners stay in their homes longer than they once did—from five years in 1985 to over thirteen years today—most first-time buyers still only live in their home between two and five years. I worry that without proper guidance, they will think too little about what their purchase has to offer. My hope is that this book has helped you appreciate that your house, be it the first or the last, can be a tool to help you achieve your larger goals in life.

The journey is not complete—not by a long shot. You've toiled to find your home. Allow it to work for you. In a way, this chapter is about home improvement, but not in the sense of making your house more beautiful. Home improvement has more than one meaning: Your dream house will return the favor. It will improve *you* emotionally, spiritually, psychologically, and even financially. It brings you to the last stage of this hero's journey, where it offers you the freedom to live your best life. Let's see how it operates.

Countdown to Launch

The American Dream doesn't end with your dream house. Were I to define the American Dream, I would say that it's the actualization of your purpose in life, brought to fruition in a country where opportunities are more abundant for more of its people than anywhere else on Earth. To that end, it's as if everything leading up to this moment was only the prequel to your true hero's journey. What is your real mission? How can your house help you achieve it?

While the United States might give you more possibilities in the pursuit of your American Dream, this is an ancient concept that long predates its founding. Folklore, mythology, and religion have always placed significant attention on the home. *Feng shui*, a body of knowledge built around channeling positive energy into your home, has existed in China for more than seven millennia. Its practices go into depth about how to arrange your rooms for prosperity, good health, and balance. Similar ideologies have appeared independently across the globe. The Greeks had their protective house deities, for instance. Every major religion, too, has its prayers and rituals surrounding the home, because we are told God is present there. Many holy books even instruct us how to buy homes and finance them ethically, and go about caring for them. We're directed to be grateful for them and build shrines within them to do so.

Taking it a step further, our contemporary mythmaking—movies—makes houses not only smart homes, but caring ones as well. Look no further than the French château in *Beauty and the Beast* or the charming, and enchanted, Casa Madrigal of *Encanto*. They are but two versions where the cups, drawers, and walls yearn for their owners' happiness and safety. Their protagonists neglect these vigilant and helpful homes at their peril. However they take shape, each of these different methods and myths emphasize the centrality of home and fortify our relationship with it.

Your home's essential purpose is to be the launch pad for the life you want to create. Acknowledge that you are more than who you are today. You were born to be a unique and powerful force in the universe. With a home you love, you cannot avoid stirring up everything else inside your heart that moves you to further growth. Beneath the din of children, television, or a contractor's saws and hammers is the answer. You could think of it as divination. The Book of Kings calls it your "still, small voice." In the framework of The Magnetic Method, the system I developed to help buyers and sellers like you, it is the culmination of its four steps—Activate, Align, Amplify, and Attract—that provide you unfettered access to your inner wisdom. By tuning in to your unique answers, you will become confident to take more risks in the service of your ever-expanding American Dream.

What do these risks look like and where could they take you? They start with the fundamental ones, like finding a significant other. My team and I have sold homes to many single professionals who had, to that point, bounced from rental to rental for years. What happens when they settle down, even for a little while? My client Darren called me not six months after closing on his one-bedroom apartment, because he had met the woman who would become his wife. It didn't hurt that he pocketed a few thousand dollars from the sale of that unit. But that home had another specific purpose—to take the pressure off. It is like the couple who cannot conceive, adopts and then gets pregnant. The things you want often wait to happen until you stop worrying about them. So, if you haven't been lucky in love yet, maybe a home purchase is the answer.

Couples who commit completely to their home search also develop much better communication skills with one another as they find the right house. My evidence is when my clients have me over after their renovations. They are house proud, without a doubt. But then I listen to buyers like Jana and Richard who navigated a yearlong renovation, only to buy the apartment upstairs and start again. If this isn't evidence of a solid relationship, what is?

To be fair, not every couple commits completely to communication, or to each other. Renovations occasionally end in a separation or divorce, and I get the unhappy news soon thereafter when they want to resell the property. But perhaps *that* was the work they needed their house to help them do.

Another client had a terrible falling-out with his company that left him financially secure, but emotionally shattered. To his astonishment, fixing up an old house in Connecticut gave him a peace of mind that he had not been able to find anywhere else. Nicole Curtis, the host of HGTV's *Rehab Addict*, put it like this in her 2016 book *Better Than New*: "More than once, a dilapidated house that I've restored has actually helped save me, and given me a path to restoring the structure of my life." As you put a home together, it may do the same to you.

🏠 🏠 🏠

Your home is also your entrepreneurial incubator. Apple, Amazon, Google, and Microsoft all started their lives in garages, as did no small share of famous bands. Billion-dollar ideas come in the shower. Bestselling novels blossom in the bedroom. Breweries take the plunge by fermenting yeast in the basement. Would-be commercial bakers unleash their creativity in the most basic of home kitchens.

Don't discount your home as a business partner. Remember Teddy, the buyer whose expectations I horribly mismanaged in the last chapter? He couldn't stop his home from helping his business. The focus groups he gathered there were much more popular than those he hosted at other event spaces. So popular, in fact, that his business took over the apartment until it outgrew his fabulous and comfortable living room. The cottage usually comes before the industry.

You might leave your company to found your own instead. Billy sold his Midtown apartment and moved to the Westchester town of Scarsdale. I have no doubt that his new home gave him the confidence to establish what grew into one of the most successful financial public relations firms in America. You could argue that for these successful people, their houses were not the cause of the prosperity in their lives, but a symptom of it. I say that it is a partnership. Does it serve you to believe otherwise?

In a 2013 interview, Oprah Winfrey described how her home became her partner too:

> You grow into a deeper, more thoughtful version of who you are. Your need to please falls away and what is left is the blessed realization that you really don't have anything to prove to anyone . . . You opt for muted tones that flow from one room to the next, you choose the sofa that makes you want to curl up with a good book on a Sunday afternoon, and create a space that makes your friends stop remarking on the exquisite art and start talking the night away. You let go of the cold stone floors that felt wrong from the start, and at long last you come home to floors made of old oak, floors that feel warm beneath your feet and bring peace and joy with every step forward you take.

Creating a home that is authentically yours is often about subtraction, not addition. Venus Williams, among the best female tennis players of all time, distilled her home life to the basics amid a surprising five-year comeback. She was quoted as saying, "It's always a dream house until you realize you don't want all the things you dreamed. Why am I doing this? I just want a closet and a gym." You don't need new art, fancy design, or a special location to create a foundation upon which your ideas will come to life either. A wealth of positivity will flood out, if you would just stop to see what is already there.

Work, from Home

Hinduism frames life as a four-stage system called *asrama*. Its second stage is that of a *gṛhastha*, or householder, encompassing life's most intense period. While we've mostly concerned ourselves with buying a home, *having* a home will eventually teach you what Hindus have known for millennia: You may be the hero of your story, but there comes a time when it's not about you anymore. This can mean getting married and having children, or starting and growing businesses. Yet ownership changes you further. It sends out a wholly new signal to your neighbors and your town, not only that you're different than you were, but committed to something bigger already. You'll be wonderfully speechless at how your community opens up to you. People come out of the woodwork because they sense that commitment. In turn, you might create community too. Because this relationship with your home allows you to serve others.

Happy homes are contagious. As they say, charity starts within them. My friend Julian, a doctor in Alabama, took that advice literally. He found that in the early mornings, the tree house in his backyard became a place of solitude and contemplation. He started opening his home for Bible study once a week, then twice a week. His home became a place where troubled youth went for counseling and consolation. I am convinced that Julian and his wife's community service also led to the wild success of his medical practice.

Claire Segeren and Cal Hunter accidentally won the wrong lot in a house auction in Scotland. Only after they bought the house did their bidding mistake come to light. Yet this dilapidated house helped them achieve a great deal. Hundreds of thousands of people flocked to their social media photos, inspired to either chip in with ideas or rebuild their own homes on similar shoestring budgets. The house became a volunteering hub for dozens of would-be do-it-yourselfers, through which they got trained on construction techniques and took new skills back to their own projects. Claire, Cal, and anyone involved got more from that home than they could ever have given. It changed the trajectory of everyone's lives for the better.

This is the true meaning of the phrase *forever home* you hear bandied about. It's not something money can buy, and it doesn't sit at the top rung of anyone's property ladder. You don't have to wait for years to find it either. That starter home can, in a way, be your forever home. Because this is not just a place, but an idea. Your forever home is the legacy you want to leave behind. It grows in size as you get clearer and clearer about the unique gifts you have to offer the world. This home or another does its share to transform you into the very best version of yourself. It's a practice that never stops. Doesn't that sound like work you'd want to take up today? So open your heart and open your house. Turn it into a hub for volunteering. Host events and fundraisers for family and friends. Make your house a reflection of the high-quality life you want to live.

Even better, when you lean in to the opportunities your new home offers, there is a wonderful side effect. Just as some of the homes you toured during your search had an ineffable "good vibe," you, too, are filling your home with positive spiritual and emotional energy. Its impact is more than energetic, however. Agents and other transaction-oriented real estate books might tell you to think about resale value, and the investments and improvements that will multiply your sale price down the road. But when your home hums at the frequency of appreciation, it begets the kind of appreciation that will simply show up in your bank account later. With every good deed, you add equity too.

There's No Place Like Home

What do you think about all the people you've read about here? I hope you were able to have some compassion for them, because you have become one of them. Your experience could never be a carbon copy, but I am sure your story will have echoes of theirs.

I offered you a few warnings when we set out on this adventure together. Specifically, that there would be awkward conversations. That you would be mightily challenged to keep your head on straight. That reality television is an exceptionally poor substitute for reality. And that you should absolutely reach out for and expect help from the unknown.

I also told you to expect that the biggest impediment to success was going to be you, and all of your excited, skeptical, doubtful, anxious, afraid, angry, and mistrustful parts. Was I right? Most importantly, did you finally understand why there could never be any shortcut to finding your home? Because, in the end, the home isn't even the point. The pursuit of home is but the structure, the housing if you will, for your journey of self-discovery. It is possible to make things better, one house at a time.

Maybe you found your search easier than I hyped it up to be. If that was the case, you should thank yourself, not me, for the inner work you have already done. Your talk therapy or book clubs. Your visits with spiritual leaders. Your recovery meetings. Your journaling or self-help programs or favorite tell-it-like-it-is podcasts. Anything that has broken through old patterns and healed the wounds of your life has served you admirably. What about your newfound peace of mind, exhilaration, freedom, or satisfaction? You have earned it. And the best part was, after all of that work, you just needed to let your house be delivered to your doorstep.

None of this takes away from the fact that, regardless of any lingering concerns about hiring an agent, real estate will always be a joint venture. Be confident that you are well-equipped to make informed decisions about every dimension of homebuying, including whom you hire to represent and advise you.

You will need that confidence, for there is a reckoning in the real estate industry underway. Dissatisfaction with the process has already come to a head with a flurry of recent class action lawsuits that question agents' motives and even assert commission collusion within different housing markets. Settlements of these lawsuits, and the regulation and legislation they spur on, will undoubtedly bring some level of upheaval to how the real estate industry does business. What you have done through reading this book, and doing its exercises, is take large steps to shield yourself from any changes that roil the current model of buying and selling homes.

I want to say goodbye on an uplifting note and congratulate you again for everything you've done. Those who prepare themselves for buying or selling a home as you have will be doing their part to improve the industry and improve the experience for all buyers. And as expectations rise, agents must, in turn, raise their game. They, too, must become better informed. They must become more thoughtful advisors. They must more thoroughly earn your trust. These shifts may ultimately prompt a new generation of more caring professionals to enter the industry. As it is, I regularly interact with a cohort of amazing agents already working today across the country. And there is another large segment of agents who at least know that you deserve the quality of service I have described here. The rest will have to learn in other, less agreeable ways.

I want nothing more than for this book to be the start of a different conversation about real estate. I pray that it becomes the antidote to everyone's obsessive attention to the money in a transaction, to the unbelievably bad behavior of buyers and sellers, to the crassness and materialism of agents on television. None of it is necessary, most of it is counterproductive, and little of it is real. You don't have to stand for it. And you certainly don't have to watch shows that promote it.

There may be a next time, or this home may truly become your forever home. Whichever it is, I wish you lots of good fortune while you're in it. My bigger hope for you is that you have found a home so wonderful that whenever you walk in, you'll feel its warm embrace. And that this very different, soul-sustaining experience of buying a home will serve as the standard for whatever life projects you take on next.

You have the keys. Now go pursue your home, and make your American Dream come true.

ACKNOWLEDGMENTS

You can't find a home without help, and you certainly can't write a book about finding a home without a lot of help either. Stacey Glick at Dystel, Goderich & Bourret was the perfect sounding board and advocate. I offer a bear hug to Matt Holt at Matt Holt Books for taking a chance on this first-time author. My editors, Katie Dickman and Lydia Choi, could not have been more constructive, or gentle, in pushing me to improve the book. Michele Matrisciani and DeAnna Acker also deserve sincere thanks for shaping the book proposal and the manuscript in its early days.

Aldous Huxley once wrote, "Visions are never our personal property." Liel Leibovitz understood the vision of what I was going for long before I did. Lisa Sandell pushed me out of the nest with love. I will be forever grateful for their support. Dan Steinman's offhand comment during lunch a few years ago set this whole project in motion, and his never-ending optimism was contagious, even as he waded courageously through primordial versions of the writing. Jared Rosen energetically shoved me toward something that resembled a book outline. Andy Nieman and MZ Goodman asked critically important questions, and offered superb feedback and ideas. Dr. David Waters has been reading my work with unbridled enthusiasm since I was 15;

this go-round was no exception. Burt Weissbourd offered tough love and much-needed perspective in his draft reviews, as did Charles Guarino and Roy Fenichel. And a special shout-out to Sam Siegel for his mind-blowingly brilliant observations. He may have missed his calling as a professional editor.

Others filled in holes in the real estate landscape. Dr. Ann Sloan Devlin served up her mastery of environmental psychology on a platter. Chad Tongue decoded Nielsen's television data. Robert Guarino (no relation to Charles) reminded me what restaurant hospitality should be. A host of real estate developers, who all wanted to remain anonymous, graciously explained the incredible and intricate work they do. Real estate professionals across the country, many of them friends, shared their buyer and seller stories and proved their genius in seeing those deals across the finish line. These include Connie Dornan in Chicago; Matt Kelly in Augusta, Georgia; Lisa Weissman in Scarsdale and Julie Alcee in White Plains, New York; Lyndsi Sitcov in Washington, D.C.; Stacy Shailendra in Atlanta; and Gary Lazarus and Keith Adler in New Orleans. I am also grateful to the home-buyers and experts I have interviewed either for this book or for my podcast. Those conversations made this book infinitely better.

I would not have had the energy and freedom to breathe life into this book without Karen Leonardi and the other members of my real estate team, nor would I have had a place to test out its ideas. Julian Billings was a spiritual touchstone throughout its writing. John Mark Shaw's care and passion has helped me make a bigger impact in the world through real estate, this book, and beyond. And to all of my buyers and sellers, I am humbled to be a part of your lives.

Every house, and life, needs a solid foundation. That has been my family and friends. All along, I kept Jason Pettigrew in my thoughts. He surely has been watching this project get built from his drafting desk in the sky. I miss him. The gentlemen of Mountain Meadows also buoyed me as the book came to life. And my running partners Stuart Birdt, Sam Jacobs, and Mike Alexander let me ramble through its thorniest parts until they made sense. To call their contribution unending patience only scratches the surface. Mike went a step further, seeing through the early mess of my writing, and commenting constructively on drafts before anyone else; I will forever mourn his untimely passing and remember his loyal friendship.

To my children, Millie, Elizabeth, and Isaac, your wonder and belief in the unseen are endlessly inspirational. I couldn't be prouder to be your father. To my wife, Sara: None of this works without you holding me and our beautiful life together. Thank you for letting me disappear on so many early mornings and weekends to see this project through to its end. Thank you for telling it like it is. Thank you for always believing in me. I love you. And one more thing: God—I am blessed beyond measure. Thank you for all of these miracles and gifts.

APPENDIX

"The Long Journey home need not
be compounded by confusion."
—Mildred Constantine, curator,
The Museum of Modern Art, 1967

The Pursuit of Home

Balance Sheet Template

Assets

- Cash: _____
- Non-Retirement Investments: _____
- Retirement Investments: _____
- Accounts Receivable (Money Owed to You): _____
- Other Assets: _____

Total Assets: _____

Additional Resources

- Money Available to Borrow from Yourself: _____
- Money Available from Family & Friends: _____

Total Resources: _____

Total Assets & Additional Resources Combined: _____

Liabilities

Current Liabilities:
- Accounts Payable: _____
- Short-Term Debt (Credit Cards, Etc.):   _____
- Long-Term Debt (Mortgages, Student Loans):   _____

                 Total Liabilities: _____

              Net Worth (Total Assets minus

                 Total Liabilities): _____

THE PURSUIT OF HOME

Offer Feedback Tool

Section One: Overcome Opposite Mode

What I Don't Like

What I Would Love

_____   _____

_____   _____

_____   _____

_____   _____

_____   _____

_____   _____

_____   _____

Section Two: Review, Refresh & Recalibrate

Now Create Your Top 10 List. This can be anything that's important to you (location, house details, views, etc.). Write your priorities here:

1. _____   6. _____

2. _____   7. _____

3. _____   8. _____

4. _____   9. _____

5. _____   10. _____

Anything that reaches 6 out of 10 you should bid on (either formally or as a thought experiment).

Create your list of properties you're bidding on:

_____   _____

_____   _____

_____   _____

_____   _____

_____   _____

Now let's move on to the process for each property you're bidding on. It is critical to listen to what your body—not your head—is saying at each step:

Target Property: _____

The Big Hurdle: How scared are you just making the first offer? What are your concerns? Is there anything you need to do to be better prepared? What is your agent suggesting for this opening offer? Does it seem too high, or too low? Are you already worried about losing the property? Does the seller's agent seem anxious, or confident, before you even submit it? Do you sense the mood trending in one direction or the other?

Notes _____

_____

_____

_____

_____

Starting Offer Price: _____

Your Offer's Been Submitted. How do you feel about it? Are you already anxious? Are you fidgety waiting for the seller to respond to you? Are you strangely calm?

Notes _____

_____

Seller's Counteroffer Price: _____

Learnings: What have you learned from the seller's counteroffer? Any new insights about the market? How does this seller negotiate, in tiny steps or in big moves? Do they take a long time? Any insights about how to structure an offer in this market? Any surprising feedback? Is the seller more flexible than you think? Are you excited about their response? Truly disappointed at their lack of flexibility? Or do you feel nothing at all? This is the real litmus test of whether you really love a property or not.

Notes _____

_____

_____

_____

Now What? You have a decision to make: Raise your offer, wait, do nothing, or walk away. How will you feel if you lose out on this purchase? How would you feel if you lost out over a very small amount of money? If you decide to do nothing, how long will you wait? What would need to change for you to change your mind? If you aren't that into the property, it's time to move on. Think through this with your agent, your friends and family, and your significant other.

Notes _____

_____

_____

_____

If you decide to make a new offer or stay firm: Buyer Counteroffer #1

_____

Rinse and Repeat. Do you feel you're moving toward a deal that you like? Are you feeling a growing sense of confidence? Or are you getting less interested in the property?

Notes _____

_____

_____

_____

Whatever you decide to do: There are going to be takeaways from every offer you make, even if you lose out in a bidding war. Did you and your significant other agree on this property? If you did, do you feel more confident about your homebuying experience? Do you feel your agent is guiding you correctly? Are you more educated about the market? Do you need to adjust your Top 10 List? Has something become more important? Has something fallen off the list? Are you surprised at what you've discovered? Make sure to capture all of your learnings!

Any Additional Notes _____

_____

_____

_____

_____

_____

Sample Agreement
(Before Times Get Tough)

INSERT TODAY'S DATE

To Whom It May Concern:

Here are the three people with whom I/we will share the important details about our home search:

1. _____

2. _____

3. _____

I/we agree to turn to these three people when we get concerned about finances, other people's behavior, or anything that freaks me/us out for support, perspective, advice, and guidance before making any big decisions.

I/we also agree to only turn to these trusted people, and not people who we know are going to be unhelpful, or worse, as we go about our home search.

Signed,

_____   _____
INSERT YOUR NAME   INSERT SECOND NAME

Walk-Through Checklist

The walk-through is your opportunity—often your last—to check the condition of the home you are buying. After the closing, you can (and I hate to tell you, you surely will) identify problems, but they will be your responsibility, rather than the seller's. Does that take away the fun of what's about to happen? To keep yourself calm, adopt this motto: *Hope for the best, prepare for the worst.*

You may have already done an inspection of a home early in the process, or a pre-pre-closing walk-through. Either of these may have generated a list of items that a seller agreed to repair, known sometimes as an *inspection contingency* or a *punch list.* If the seller had agreed to make the repairs, this walk-through serves to ensure that the repairs are up to your standards and include quality work.

For that reason, it's important to do a thorough investigation of the property, perhaps the most detailed look you'll ever give your house! Make sure there aren't any new issues, or remaining issues that the seller was supposed to address and did not. Do not take the seller's word that everything's in good working order—check for yourself. Even if you are buying the home as is, write down what needs to be replaced or repaired. This will make it easier to fix up your home later.

Unless a seller has pre-negotiated staying in the home post-closing, you want to make sure they are completely moved out of the home before you close. Walking through an empty home makes it much easier to spot new defects that may have occurred when the seller was moving out, as well as repairs that weren't completed as agreed. If the seller is staying on, you'll likely have an arrangement to do a second walk-through when they are gone.

Note: You might want to close off each room as you check to ensure that you don't duplicate your work. Or, as a carpenter might say: Measure twice and cut once. Is it worth walking through each room twice so you don't miss anything? That's your call.

Preparing for the Walk-Through

What Should You Ask For?

Ask the seller for the warranties or repair receipts for all the work they did on the home. Ask for login information (username and password) for any smart-home technology. Ask for contact information for specialists too. Are there people who know the house? That is, who has the seller called in case something breaks again after you move in? This can save you money, as most home repair companies offer the seller limited-time warranties that may still include free fixes.

Is your seller leaving replacement lights, extra floor tiles, paint colors, or cans with paint in them? Any other extra items from their renovations? Going that extra mile is a free thing that a seller can do to generate a lot of goodwill at a stressful time.

What Did the Sellers Agree To?

Review your documents over the course of the buying process. What did the sellers agree to leave behind? What did they agree to repair?

What Should You Bring?

Bring along copies of all of these documents:

❑ Home inspection summaries
❑ Inspection contingency

- ❑ Punch list
- ❑ Any other documents that list every repair the seller agreed to complete
- ❑ Measuring tape
- ❑ Phone for recording photos and/or video of issues
- ❑ Phone charger to check power outlets
- ❑ Pen or pencil to cross out every item on your final walk-through checklist
- ❑ This list

What to Look for During the Walk-Through

Leftover Items

- ❑ Look in every room to check for any belongings that the seller left behind. Items might be: leftover toys, old paint cans, lawn equipment, cleaning supplies. Don't forget to look in the closets (every drawer!), attic, basement, and any garages or sheds.

HVAC: Air-Conditioning and Heat

- ❑ Turn on as soon as you arrive, to make sure it's functioning properly—in both heat and A/C modes.
- ❑ Make sure you have remote controls to any air-conditioning units.
- ❑ Make sure any smart-home items are working—and that you have logins!

Floors

- ❑ Are the floors clean and broom-swept?
- ❑ Do you see any evidence of termites, rodents, ants, or garbage the seller left behind? If you see signs of infestation, call an exterminator before closing.
- ❑ Look for mouse droppings, bite marks on wood, and other signs of uninvited critters. Anything that might have been covered by furniture should be noted; you're usually protected in your contract if a seller accidentally or

purposely hid issues. Note: Dry rot, spongy floors, and wooden walls that look like they're covered in tiny pinholes can all be signs of termites.

❏ Any floor damage from the seller's move-out? Any discoloration or issues under rugs that you couldn't see before?

Walls

❏ Have the sellers removed anything that should have remained?

❏ Was art removed and treated appropriately? Usually holes cannot be larger than a certain size before a seller would be required to repair the wall.

❏ Are TVs removed or kept in place, as per your contract?

❏ While we're on the walls—don't forget to inspect the chimney. Birds and raccoons don't wait long to take up residence inside chimneys after sellers move out.

Ceiling

❏ Any ceiling-mounted projectors removed as expected?

❏ Are all smoke/CO_2 detectors present and working? Test them.

Lights

❏ Any flickers?

❏ Any lights out?

❏ Are all light fixtures in place or replaced appropriately?

Kitchen

- Appliances
  ❏ Turn on your oven. Make sure it heats up without smelling like gas.
  ❏ Run the dishwasher through a full cycle.
  ❏ Check the water in the refrigerator.

- ❑ Check the icemaker for functionality.
- ❑ Run the garbage disposal if the home has one.
- Cabinets and Drawers
  - ❑ Anything still in there that shouldn't be?
  - ❑ Do they open and close?
  - ❑ Open sink cabinets and check for mold (around your sinks as well).

Other Appliances

- ❑ Washing machine: Run a cycle.
- ❑ Dryer: Turn on and off and make sure it heats up.
- ❑ Check any bathroom floor heating systems for functionality.

Plumbing

- ❑ Run water in all the drains to make sure they empty out and don't clog.
- ❑ Make sure there aren't any strange smells coming from the running water.
- ❑ Inspect for leaks and water pressure.
- ❑ Flush every single toilet to make sure it works well and refills.
- ❑ Verify that the water shutoff valves near the base of the toilets also work.
- ❑ Run the water in your showers and sinks. Make sure the water gets hot and cold in a reasonable amount of time.
- ❑ Check the water pressure in the shower.
- ❑ Confirm that your bathtub holds water when you plug the drain.
- ❑ Check for mold. Pay special attention to toilet bases and the drain of your bathtub or shower.

Alarms

- ❑ Arm and disarm the home's security system if it has one.
- ❑ If your home is equipped with an alarm system that tells you when a window or exterior door is open, arm the alarm and make sure the sensors on all of your doors and windows work.
- ❑ Confirm that only the correct code or key can activate the system.

Locks and Windows and Openings

❑ Do all locks work? Do you have keys to all the locks in the house?

❑ Do you have keys to any mailboxes, sheds, etc.?

❑ Do all windows and doors lock and unlock correctly? Do all windows slide open easily—and stay open? Do any windows or doors stick (major hazard in the event of a fire or other emergency)?

❑ Window screens: Are there holes, tears, or defects in the window screens? Are any missing? Do window screens pop out easily?

❑ Check windows for cracks or damage.

❑ Open and close the garage door. Make sure it operates, and only when you use the correct key or code. Make sure you have its remote, if there is one.

Electricity and Outlets

❑ Walk through the house with your cell phone charger and plug it into every outlet in every room. You don't need to wait and see if the outlet charges your phone; just ensure that your charger registers the outlet as soon as you plug it in.

❑ Check the plate covers on the electrical switches. Make sure the plates look secure and don't display any signs of damage.

❑ Confirm that the home's light fixtures and doorbells work as well.

Backyard and Outdoors

❑ Inspect the outside of the property carefully—no different from the interior.

❑ Take a walk around the lawn or backyard and make sure the landscaping looks as before. Sellers might dig up bushes, plants, and even small trees when they leave their property behind!

❑ Check any fencing for holes or other damage.

❑ If the house has a gate, make sure the gate latches and unlatches easily.

❑ Look at the home's irrigation system, if it has one. Turn the water on and off and make note of any sprinklers that aren't working. Inspect the interior and

exterior of any sheds. Confirm that the homeowner hasn't left any danger-
ous chemicals or tools lying around.

❑ Does the home have a pool? Inspect it to look for mold, mildew, and damage to the lining. Test and inspect the pool gate. Take notes of any damage.

If You Find Issues During the Walk-Through

What if you find issues during your walk-through?

❑ Take photos of the issue.

❑ Shoot video of the issue. Slow running water, malfunctioning electronics, etc.

❑ If need be, measure the size of the issue.

❑ Point the issue out to your real estate agent.

❑ Make sure that the seller or seller's agent sees the issue as well and acknowl-
edges it.

❑ Send an email to your attorney or agent with the specific issue described,
and attach photos or videos if applicable.

How to Resolve the Issues You Find

Here are some of the options. They depend upon the significance of what you find:

- **Fix the issue:** Ask the seller to fix it before the closing.
- **Delay the closing:** Give the seller time to fix the problem.
- **Ask for credit:** Withhold money from the seller's proceeds, to pay for
  repairs after the closing.
- **Walk away or take legal action:** Only in the most extreme situations would
  you even consider this option. Think major damage or a hugely expensive
  repair that a seller remains unwilling to address. This is exceedingly rare.

You'll want to speak with your real estate agent, attorney, and even your
close friends to determine how you want to proceed. Be strategic, patient, and
methodical. Don't forget that you love this house, and don't let the walk-through
walk all over you.

NOTES

Chapter 1

p. 9   *Image* A Cape Cod House

p. 11   *It is reliably ranked among the most traumatic* https://www
.sciencedirect.com/science/article/abs/pii/S0165178116309799.

p. 12   *same redemption 'is hidden within us all. . . .'* Joseph Campbell, *The Hero with a Thousand Faces* (New York: Pantheon, 1949).

p. 14   *more people are using real estate agents* Kelsey Ramirez, "More Americans Are Using Real Estate Agents Than Ever Before," Housingwire, November 12, 2018, https://www.housingwire.com
/articles/47376-more-americans-are-using-real-estate-agents-than
-ever-before/.

p. 14   *fewer buyers and sellers are rosy* Melissa Dittmann Tracey, "Buyer's Remorse is Rampant Among Pandemic Purchasers," *Realtor Magazine* January 23, 2023, https://www.nar.realtor/magazine
/real-estate-news/sales-marketing/buyers-remorse-is-rampant
-among-pandemic-purchasers.

p. 14   *Adding to this remorse and dissatisfaction* "Homebuying Sentiment Hits New Survey Low," Fannie Mae, June 6, 2024, https://
www.fanniemae.com/newsroom/fannie-mae-news/homebuying
-sentiment-hits-new-survey-low.

p. 14 *Half of all apartments in the United States are owned* Carol Ryan, "Welcome to the Neighborhood! Wall Street Designed It," *Wall Street Journal*, January 3, 2024, https://www.wsj.com/finance /investing/welcome-to-the-neighborhood-wall-street-designed-it -70562612.

p. 14 *Investment funds could own* Will Parker, "Wall Street Has Spent Billions Buying Homes. A Crackdown Is Looming," *Wall Street Journal*, April 29, 2024, https://www.wsj.com/real-estate /wall-street-has-spent-billions-buying-homes-a-crackdown-is -looming-f85ae5f6.

p. 14 *Nearly a third* Rachel Louise Ensign, "Boomers Bought Up the Big Homes. Now They're Not Budging," *Wall Street Journal*, April 13, 2024, https://www.wsj.com/economy/housing/baby -boomers-big-homes-real-estate-inventory-3a047cb6.

p. 14 *Aren't hitting the market* Laurel Wamsley, "Many Baby Boomers Own Homes That Are Too Big. Can They Be Enticed to Sell Them?" NPR, April 18, 2024, https://www.npr.org/2024 /04/18/1244171720/baby-boomers-large-houses-millennials -homeownership.

p. 20 *Average home price in America is, as of 2023* Amy Fontinelle, "Median Home Price by State," Forbes Advisor, May 7, 2024, https://www.forbes.com/advisor/mortgages/real-estate/median -home-prices-by-state/.

Chapter 2

p. 23 *Image* Craftsman House

p. 31 *"If you long for something"* Mary Morrissey, "How to Be Successful: Here's the Secret," April 16, 2019, *Brave Thinking Institute Blog*, https://www.bravethinkinginstitute.com/blog/life -transformation/how-to-be-successful.

p. 32   *the dilemma is on* Love It or List It Meghan Shouse, "Who Won Most Often on *Love It or List It*?" *House Beautiful*, December 5, 2023, https://www.housebeautiful.com/lifestyle/entertainment /a46040704/who-won-most-love-it-or-list-it/.

p. 32   *"When you look back"* Michael Singer, *The Untethered Soul*, p. 118

Chapter 3

p. 42   *"We celebrate Independence Day"* Barbara Kingsolver: Interview, Emory & Henry College Literary Festival, September 30, 2011.

p. 43   *Image* A Split-level Ranch, the classic of suburban life.

p. 44   *"Zillow Therapy"* Elizabeth Bernstein, "Pretend Renovations, Houses You'll Never Buy: Call It Zillow Therapy," *Wall Street Journal*, June 30, 2024, https://www.wsj.com/lifestyle/zillow -therapy-new-home-9bb6cd93.

p. 47   *Interviewed only one agent* "Quick Real Estate Statistics," National Association of Realtors, July 7, 2024, https://www.nar .realtor/research-and-statistics/quick-real-estate-statistics.

p. 49   *Mapped out why he thought real estate brokers* Jimmy Burgess, "7 IMPORTANT Reasons Real Estate Agents Will Always Be Needed," YouTube, https://www.youtube.com/watch?v=mND kSZxEAxE.

p. 58   *Myers–Briggs personality test* https://www.myersbriggs.org/my -mbti-personality-type/the-16-mbti-personality-types/.

p. 62   *Almost half of homebuyers are Homebodies* Estimates on Buyer Personalities in the population (10% Designers, 50% Meter Readers, etc.) were inspired by the research done by Jeremie Kubicek and Steve Cockram's *5 Voices: How to Communicate Effectively with Everyone You Lead*, Wiley, 2016.

p. 74 *A recent Zillow study reported* Jim Dalrymple II, "Majority of buyers lean on agents, not banks, for financing info: Poll," Inman, May 23, 2023, https://www.inman.com/2023/05/23/majority-of -buyers-lean-on-agents-not-banks-for-financing-info-poll/.

p. 75 *The average Realtor only works* "Highlights from the NAR Member Profile," National Association of Realtors, https://www .nar.realtor/research-and-statistics/research-reports/highlights -from-the-nar-member-profile#income.

p. 75 *Real estate agents who defined themselves* Gary Farris, "Real Estate as a Part-Time Job: Can You Be a Part-Time Real Estate Agent?" Calibri Real Estate, October 6, 2024, https://www .colibrirealestate.com/career-hub/real-estate-salary/real-estate -salary-part-time-real-estate-agent-salary-why-testing-the-water -may-be-safer-than-diving-in-full-time/.

Chapter 4

p. 78 *"Welcome to my house!"* Bram Stoker, *Dracula*, chapter 2.

p. 79 *Image* A Victorian House (or a vampire's mansion?)

p. 80 *Comedian John Mulaney described* John Mulaney, "The Comeback Kid" Netflix Special, 2015.

p. 84 *Status-seeking through the homes we own* David Nadelle, "6 Reasons 93% of Homebuyers Have Regrets About Purchasing a House in 2023," Yahoo!finance, August 8, 2023, https://finance .yahoo.com/news/6-reasons-93-homebuyers-regrets-173511177 .html.

p. 84 *Maslow's hierarchy of needs* A note: As I thought about it, Maslow's hierarchy of needs struck me as only partially helpful, and an ultimately incomplete framework for the house search. See Saul McLeod, PhD, "Maslow's Hierarchy of Needs," SimplyPsychology, January 24, 2024, https://www.simplypsychology.org/maslow.html.

p. 85   *Author Karal Ann Marling* Karal Marling, *Designing Disney's Theme Parks: The Architecture of Reassurance*, (Flammarion, 1998).

p. 85   *You have been exposed to between 4,000 and 10,000 advertisements* Nadia, "How Many Ads Do We See a Day?" siteefy, August 29, 2024, https://siteefy.com/how-many-ads-do-we-see-a-day.

p. 86   *The now-ubiquitous "open concept house"* Garcia-Navarro and Kaysen conversation, https://www.distractify.com/p/why-hgtv-homes-are-all-open-concept.

p. 87   *Nearly 44 million view its programming per month* "Beyond Big Data: The Audience Watching over the Air," Nielsen, January 2024, https://www.nielsen.com/insights/2024/beyond-big-data-the-audience-watching-over-the-air/.

p. 87   *"Every human being is hypnotized"* Maxwell Maltz, *Psycho-Cybernetics*, p. 60.

p. 90   *Courtroom judges* Kurt Kleiner, "Lunchtime Leniency: Judges' Rulings Are Harsher When They Are Hungrier," *Scientific American*, September 2011, https://www.scientificamerican.com/article/lunchtime-leniency/.

p. 92   *More likely to land in the suburbs* https://www.huduser.gov/portal/pdredge/pdr-edge-frm-asst-sec-080320.html and https://www.pewresearch.org/short-reads/2018/10/02/5-facts-about-u-s-suburbs/

p. 92   *Environmental psychologist Ann Sloan Devlin* Ann Sloan Devlin, *What Americans Build and Why* (New York: Cambridge University Press, 2010), 23.

p. 92   Devlin, 21.

p. 93   *Creating mental fatigue* Ruth Garside, "Attention Restoration Theory: A Systematic Review," European Centre for Environment & Human Health, University of Exeter, https://www.ecehh.org/research/attention-restoration-theory-a-systematic-review/.

p. 93 *Too-tall neighborhood hedges* Katinka H. Evensen, et al., "Testing the Effect of Hedge Height on Perceived Safety—A Landscape Design Intervention," *Sustainability*, April 30, 2021, https://pub.epsilon.slu.se/24410/1/evensen_k_h_et_al_210607.pdf.

p. 93 *The separate dining room is going extinct* Maggie Eastland, "Goodbye Bathtub and Living Room. America's Homes Are Shrinking," *Wall Street Journal*, August 22, 2023, https://www.wsj.com/economy/housing/home-prices-mortgage-rates-smaller-houses-34e06123.

p. 93 *Culturally speaking* Aurelie Saulton, et al., "Cultural Differences in Room Size Perception," *PLOS One*, on National Library of Medicine website, April 20, 2017, https://www.ncbi.nlm.nih.gov/pmc/articles/PMC5398688/.

p. 94 *70% of homebuyers are a couple* "Highlights from the Profile of Home Buyers and Sellers," National Association of Realtors, .https://www.nar.realtor/research-and-statistics/research-reports/highlights-from-the-profile-of-home-buyers-and-sellers.

p. 94 *Tolle puts it beautifully* Tolle, *Stillness Speaks*, chapter 6.

p. 95 *On the perils of following your bliss* Russ Roberts, in discussing his 2022 book *Wild Problems* on Tim Ferriss's podcast, started my thinking of decision making as a retrospective process. https://tim.blog/2022/08/07/russ-roberts-transcript/.

p. 96 Maslow, *The Third Force*, 1970, p. 90.

p. 104 *The "great mother art"* Frank Lloyd Wright, *An Organic Architecture: The Architecture of Democracy* (Lund Humphries, 1939).

p. 105 *Began its life as a* spec house "Number of Homes in the United States in 2021, by Age," Statista, May 24, 2024. https://www.statista.com/statistics/1042458/home-age-usa/.

p. 105 *You have no free will* I will leave the broader topic of whether we have free will at all to philosophers and other public thinkers like Sam Harris.

Chapter 5

p. 106 *Rumi* "The Guest House" by Jalaluddin Rumi, a 13th-century Persian poet and Sufi mystic.

p. 107 *Image* A Greek Revival House (or a fraternity house, perhaps)

p. 120 *Get help from family for their purchase* Abha Bhattarai and Federica Cocco, *Washington Post*, May 27, 2024, "What does it take to buy a house? Increasingly, Mom and Dad," https://www .washingtonpost.com/business/2024/05/19/home-buyers-parents -help-housing-affordability/.

Chapter 6

p. 128 *"The place in which I'll fit will not exist until I make it"* James Baldwin, 1957 letter to Sol Stein, published in Stein's 2004 book, *Native Sons: A Friendship That Created One of the Greatest Works of the 20th Century: Notes of a Native Son.*

p. 129 *Image* A New York City Brownstone

p. 132 *"thought worms"* Anne Craig, "Discovery of 'Thought Worms' Opens Window to the Mind," *Queen's Gazette*, July 13, 2020, https://www.queensu.ca/gazette/stories/discovery-thought -worms-opens-window-mind.

p. 132 *Inclined to focus on negative experiences* Vaish A. Grossmann, et al., "Not All Emotions Are Created Equal: The Negativity Bias in Social-Emotional Development," *Psychological Bulletin*, on APA PsycNet website, https://psycnet.apa.org/doiLanding ?doi=10.1037%2F0033-2909.134.3.383, and on National Library of Medicine website, https://pmc.ncbi.nlm.nih.gov/articles/PMC 3652533/.

p. 132 *"When your body and mind are both living in the past"* Lewis Howes, "How to Overcome Negative Emotions, Let Go of Your

Identity, and Truly Love Yourself," January 4, 2021, https://lewis
howes.com/podcast/how-to-overcome-negative-emotions-let
-go-of-your-identity-and-truly-love-yourself-with-dr-joe-dispenza
-part-2/.

p. 133   *"Martin Luther King didn't have a dream"* Richard Williams,
a.k.a. Prince EA, "Everybody Dies, But Not Everybody Lives,"
https://www.youtube.com/watch?v=ja-n5qUNRi8.

p. 134   *The impact of commitment* W. H. Murray, *The Scottish Hima-
layan Expedition*, 1951, Chapter 1, p. 7.

p. 135   *Introduced himself as Zito* Antony Zito's wonderful work is
still on public display in Manhattan and Connecticut and for sale
online: https://zitogallery.com/.

p. 136   *"clear or obvious to the eye"* Google "manifest definition" and
you'll see the same definition I found.

p. 140   *Diplomatic advisor Tal Becker* Dan Senor's *Call Me Back*
podcast, October 14, 2024, "One Year Since October 7th."

p. 144   *On being kind versus being nice* Sam Jacobs and his book
Kind Folks Finish First inspired this framing.

Chapter 7

p. 146   *"The home is not the one tame place"* G. K. Chesterton, "On
Certain Modern Writers and the Institution of the Family," in *Her-
etics*, 1905.

p. 147   *Image* A Colonial

p. 148   *Bob Proctor's house-oriented analogy* Bob Proctor, from his
1992 program, "Your Winner's Image."

p. 154   *Dark night of the soul* St. John of the Cross, 16th century
poem, "La Noche Oscura del Alma."

p. 156   *Be discriminated against when compared* More on unmarried couples being discriminated against: "Caveat Co-ops!" Lucas Ferrara, February 2006, https://cooperatornews.com/article/caveat-co-ops.

p. 162   On over-asking-price offers: Some have suggested, and I concede, that these kinds of brown-nosing letters might be discriminatory. For some buyers, that may even be the point. It could be an unintentional violation of fair housing laws, especially if sellers choose families over buyers without children, buyers from certain religious groups, or just people who look like them.

p. 164   *On* premeditatio malorum He did write this in his masterwork, *Meditations.*

p. 164   *Psychologist Gary Klein called this a "pre-mortem"* Gary Klein, "Performing a Project Premortem," *Harvard Business Review*, September 1, 2007.

Chapter 8

p. 166   *"A man travels the world over"* George Moore, *The Brook Kerith*, 1916.

p. 167   *Image* A Tudor-style house

p. 171   *More than 20% of closings are delayed* "Realtors® Confidence Index Survey," National Association of Realtors, April 2021, https://www.nar.realtor/sites/default/files/documents/REALTOR_Confidence_Index_052021.pdf.

p. 171   *Roughly 5% of pending offers fall through* Richard Haddad, "How Often Do Pending Offers Fall Through When Selling a Home?" HomeLight, February 9, 2024, https://www.homelight.com/blog/how-often-do-pending-offers-fall-through/.

p. 183   "renovation," Online Etymology Dictionary, https://www
.etymonline.com/word/renovation.

p. 184   *Tony Robbins and Dean Graziosi self-help program* Graziosi
claims to have learned it from Joe Stump, a mentor of his. It's an
old, and wonderful, idea. You can find it in many places online.

Chapter 9

p. 188   *"Home is where your story begins"* Attributed to Annie Danielson and her home design work.

p. 189   *Image* The San Remo on Central Park West in Manhattan,
a classic apartment house that looks a little like a rocket ship.

p. 190   *Prioritizing homeownership for nearly two centuries* I should
acknowledge that housing laws, lending programs, and even lending institutions have not always helped everyone evenly in the
past. But we as a country have come a long way in correcting these
wrongs.

p. 190   *Other towns' very names* If schools and institutions can be
renamed because we no longer like the people they once honored,
why can't we rename towns that seem so downright depressing?

p. 194   *Most first-time home buyers still only live in their home* Susan
Meyer, "Average Length of Homeownership: Americans Spend
Less Than 15 Years in One Home," Zebra, March 11, 2024,
https://www.thezebra.com/resources/home/average-length-of
-homeownership.

p. 196   1 Kings 19:11-13.

p. 198   *Oprah Winfrey described how her home* Oprah Winfrey,
"How Oprah Found a Home Decorating Style That Spoke to Her,"
Oprah Daily, January 31, 2022, https://www.oprahdaily.com/life
/a38876138/oprah-home-decorating-style-california/.

p. 198   *Venus Williams . . . quoted as saying* Roxanne Roberts, "Game, Set, Matching Ottomans: Venus Williams Turns from Tennis to Interior Design," *Washington Post*, November 6, 2014, https://www .washingtonpost.com/lifestyle/style/game-set-matching-ottomans -venus-williams-turns-from-tennis-to-interior-design/2014/11/06 /51c45862-64f8-11e4-bb14-4cfea1e742d5_story.html.

p. 200   *Claire Segeren and Cal Hunter accidentally* Ijeoma Ndukwe, "They Accidentally Bought the Wrong House. So They Made It the Right House," *New York Times*, October 2, 2023, https:// www.nytimes.com/2023/10/02/realestate/scotland-villa-home -renovation.html.

p. 202   *A flurry of recent class action lawsuits* Debra Kamin, "Powerful Realtors Group Loses Its Grip on the Industry, " *New York Times*, December 27, 2023, https://www.nytimes.com/2023/12/27 /realestate/national-association-realtors-real-estate.html.

INDEX

ABOUT THE AUTHOR

Scott Harris is a successful residential real estate agent and entrepreneur who has marketed and sold nearly $2 billion of New York City properties in a career spanning more than two decades. He has been recognized as a Top 25 agent in New York City and among the top 200 in the nation, by sales volume, by the WSJ / RealTrends Verified™ Top 1000 list. He is regularly among the top 0.02% of Realtors nationwide, with a client roster that includes the leading lights of every industry.

In 2010, Scott founded the Harris Residential Team. It went on to become a top-ranking team among more than 2,500 agents at Brown Harris Stevens, New York City's oldest real estate brokerage firm. In 2025, Scott founded MAGNETIC, an independent firm dedicated to making dreams come true through real estate and The Magnetic Method™.

Scott has been a guest on *Good Morning America* and quoted in publications and media such as the *New York Times*, *Wall Street Journal*, *Money Magazine*, *Architectural Digest*, MSN, Yahoo! Finance, and Fox News; his listings have been featured in major print and online outlets around the globe.

Scott shares his thought leadership on the New York City real estate market and life as a New Yorker via his newsletters, social media, and now, this book. He also hosts *The Pursuit of Home with Scott Harris* real estate podcast, which features real people buying real estate, and serves up solutions to the obstacles listeners will face to get there themselves.

Scott lives on Manhattan's Upper West Side with his wife and three children.